NEW THREE GORGES
NEUE DREI SCHLUCHTEN

盧　進

中国旅游出版社
China Travel & Tourism Press
Verlag für Tourismus Chinas

目 録
Contents
INHALTVERZEICHNIS

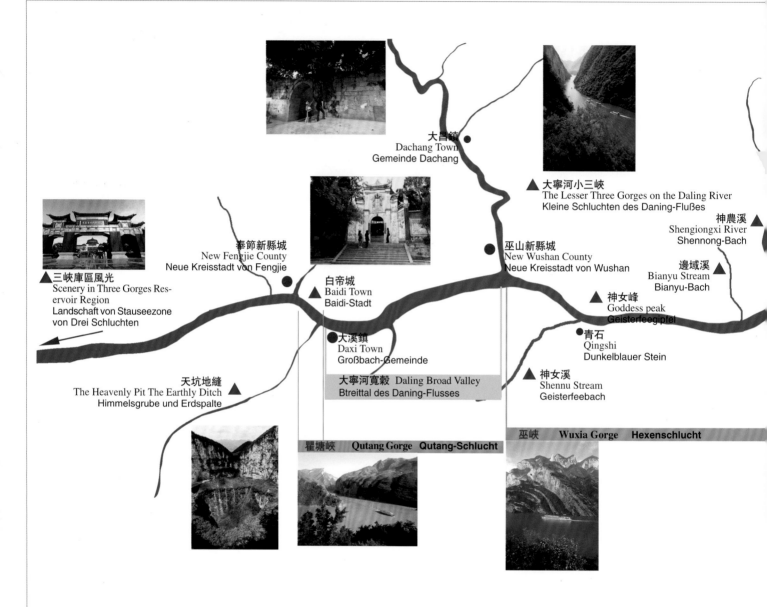

大昌鎮
Dachang Town
Gemeinde Dachang

大寧河小三峽
The Lesser Three Gorges on the Daling River
Kleine Schluchten des Daning-Flußes

神農溪
Shengiongxi River
Shennong-Bach

邊域溪
Bianyu Stream
Bianyu-Bach

奉節新縣城
New Fengjie County
Neue Kreisstadt von Fengjie

巫山新縣城
New Wushan County
Neue Kreisstadt von Wushan

神女峰
Goddess peak
Geisterfeegipfel

三峽庫區風光
Scenery in Three Gorges Reservoir Region
Landschaft von Stauseezone von Drei Schluchten

白帝城
Baidi Town
Baidi-Stadt

青石
Qingshi
Dunkelblauer Stein

大溪鎮
Daxi Town
Großbach-Gemeinde

神女溪
Shennu Stream
Geisterfeebach

天坑地縫
The Heavenly Pit The Earthly Ditch
Himmelsgrube und Erdspalte

大寧河寬穀 Daling Broad Valley
Btreittal des Daning-Flusses

瞿塘峽 Qutang Gorge Qutang-Schlucht

巫峽 Wuxia Gorge Hexenschlucht

長江三峽景點分布圖
Tourist Sketch Map of the Three Gorges
Lageplan von Sehenswüdigkeiten bei Drei Schluchten des Changjiang-Flußes

長江三峽在中國的位置圖
Geographical Position Map of the Yangtze Three Gorges in China
Lage von Drei Schluchten des Changjiang-Flußes in China

北京
Beijing

黃河
Hong River

宜昌 武漢
Yichang Wuhan

上海
Shanghai

奉節
Fengjie

重慶
Chongqing

長江三峽
The Yangtze Three Gorges

神農架
Shennongjia
Shennongjia

王昭君故裏
Wang Zhaojun's Howntown
Heimat von Wamg Zhaojun

...uKou
...dukou

屈原祠
Quyuan Town
Qu-Yuan-Tempel

香溪河
Xiangxi River
Xiangxi-Fluß

歸州鎮
Guizhou Town
Gemeinde Guizhou

...東新縣城
v Badong County
ie Kreisstadt von Badong

香溪河寬穀 XiangXi Broad Valley
reittal des Xiangxi-Flusses

屈原鎮
Quyuan Town
Qu-Yuan- Gemeinde

三峽工程
The Three Gorges Project
Sanxia- Schluchten des Changjiang-Flußzes-Projekt

九灣溪
Jiuwan Stream
Neunbogenbach

黃陵廟
Huangling Temple
Gelbgrab-Tempel

廟南寬穀 Miaonan Broad Valley
Breittal von Miaonan

三游洞
Three Visitors Cave
Höhle von Drei Reisenden

石牌峽人家
Shipai and the Eamily
of the Three Gorges

宜昌市
Yichang City
Stadt Yichang

泗溪
Sixi
Sixi-Bach

葛洲壩水利樞紐工程
Gezhouba Key Water
Conservancy Project
Gezhouba-Staudamm -
Wasserbauschlüßelprojekt

西陵峽 XIlIng Gorge WestgrabSchlucht

壯麗的新三峽

長江三峽是長江中最爲壯美雄奇和幽深秀麗的一段大峽穀，爲中國十大風景名勝。它西起重慶奉節縣的白帝城，東至湖北省宜昌市的南津關，全長近200公裏，由瞿塘峽、巫峽和西陵峽三個峽段組成，總稱爲"長江三峽"。

長江三峽是長江風景旅游線上最爲集中的山水畫廊和文明走廊，擁有着無窮的誘惑，這一大自然的杰作，猶如一部宏大的交響樂章，三段峽穀各有各的韵律，各有各的風姿，瞿塘峽雄偉傲岸，斷岩峭壁，獨樹一幟，巫峽幽深秀麗，雲纏霧繞，別具風彩，西陵峽灘險峰奇，水嘯岩吟，自成一派。峽與峽之間，還有三段江岸開闊的寬穀，極目四望，"四野縱橫千嶂裏，人烟錯雜半山中"。正如聆聽了激昂的樂章過后，讓一段委婉低回的音節淌入心臆，令人心曠神怡，歷來被許多的詩人墨客千古傳頌。

從戰國時期的屈原《橘頌》到南北朝的酈道元《水經注·江水》，其間三峽沒有改變；從唐朝的李白《早發白帝城》到宋朝的陸游《入蜀記》，其間三峽沒有改變；再到明清英國人立德所著《扁舟過三峽》，其間三峽也沒有改變，所改變的是人口的不斷增多，猿猴不斷地减少，森林不斷地喪失。建國初，自從瞿塘峽口的大灩澦堆被炸掉，便拉開新中國治理峽江的序幕，三峽中的一些險灘逐漸消失。20世紀的80年代初，由于葛洲壩工程實現了第一次長截流，使得長江三峽發生了有史以來的河湖之變。

公元2003年6月1日，舉世矚目的長江三峽工程下閘蓄水，彈指十日，滄海桑田，庫區蓄水已達海拔135米，四個月后水位又增至139米，整個長江三峽最終發生了根本性的改變，三峽已經成爲巨大的人工湖。作爲一條河流的三峽，她的原始風貌已不復存在，朝着東方奔馳了上億年的浩蕩峽江，大大地放慢了它的節奏，江水變得平緩與柔順，渾黃的江水漸漸地變成了黛綠，第一次映出了群山的倒影，告別的已經告別，新生的已經新生，一個嶄新的三峽已橫空出世！

三峽工程曾經是中國人的一個世紀之夢，然而，當今天這個夢想成真之時，我們曾經居住過的古老而美麗的生活家園却又變成了一個逝去的舊夢，世間之事，嘆難兩全。面對今天的高峽平湖，在我們復雜的情感中，也有足够的暢快和欣慰之感。三峽雖然少了奇險幽深之美，畢竟也新添了浩渺闊遠之美，最重要的是：正因爲有了三峽工程的興建，就有了今天三峽庫區内這些星落棋布的現代化新城鎮，使得三峽人能够提前至少半個世紀而融入了現代人的生活！

壯麗的新三峽，充滿着無限魅力！三峽大壩蓄水后的高峽平湖造就出許多奇麗的景觀，構成了新三峽別具魅力的山水自然，三峽之美涵養着文化、收伏着心靈，永遠值得我們一次次地去探尋，新三峽究竟有哪些迷人的風韵呢？讓我們一同走進新三峽，走進一個全新的世界！

The Splendid New Three Gorges

The Yangtze Three Gorges, the most splendid and beautiful section of the Yangtze River, is one of the 10 top sceneries in China. Beginning from Baidi Town in Fengjie, Chongqing in the west and ending in Nanjin Pass in Yichang, Hubei Province in the east, its total length is nearly 200 kilometers. The Three Gorges consists of three sections-the Qutang Gorge, the Wu Gorge and the Xiling Gorge .

Concentrating natural "landscape painting galleries" and "cultural corridors", the Yangtze Three Gorges, a masterpiece of nature , is just like a great symphony. Each of the three gorges has its unique rhyme. The Qutang Gorge is known for its majestic and overhanging precipices. The Wu Gorge is famous for its secluded beauty with clouds and mist floating slowly. The Xiling Gorge is noted for its dangerous shoals and peculiar peaks with roaring rapids. Among the gorges, there are also three broad valleys. Coming to these broad valleys after passing the narrow gorges seems to be listening to a leisurely melody after an impassioned rhapsody. It refreshes both the heart and the mind. The beautiful views attracted lots of poets and men of letters in past dynasties.

From Ode to the Orange Tree of Qu Yuan in the Warring States, to Water Scripture Comments . Rivers of Li Daoyuan in the Southern and Northern Dynasties, the Three Gorges didn't change. From Leaving Baidi Town in the Early Morning of Li Bai in the Tang Dynasty, to Notes of Going into Sichuan of Lu You in the Song Dynasty, the Three Gorges didn't change. Even to Taking A Narrow Boat Through the Three Gorges written by an Englishman Leda in the Qing Dynasty, the Three Gorges didn't change. What changed was the increasing population, the decreasing monkeys and the losing forests. At the beginning of the foundation of the P.R.C., since the Great Yanyudui Rock was exploded, the prologue of new China harnessing the Three Gorges and River was opened. Some dangerous shoals have disappeared gradually. In the early eighties of last century, because the Gezhouba Project realized the first damming of the Yangtze River, a change from river to lake in the Yangtze Three Gorges occurred within the memory of history. Early in this century, because the Three Gorges Project reserved water, a huge change, which is unimaginable as if the sea changed to a field, took place in the Yangtze Three Gorges at last.

On June 1, 2003, the world famous Yangtze Three Gorges Project started to store water. Only ten days later, the water level of the reservoir area reached 135 meters. Four months later, the water level rose to 139 meters. The Three Gorges has been a huge man-made lake and lost its original look .The Yangtze River, which runs forward with great strength and vigor for millions of years, now greatly slows its paces here. The yellow river became green and smooth. The shadows of mountains first can be clearly reflected on the water. A new Three Gorges was burn into the world!

The Three Gorges Project was once a dream of Chinese for 100 years. But now, when the dream was realized, the old beautiful homeland where we ever lived became a bygone dream. The things in the world can't satisfy both sides. But facing the smooth lake rising in the high mountains, we have a joyful and gratified sense in our complex emotions. With less peculiar and elegant beauty, the Three Gorges is now more immense. It is more important that the construction of the Three Gorges Project brought these new towns spreading all over the reservoir area and modernized the life of the people in the Three Gorges at least half a century ahead of time.

The splendid new Three Gorges is full of infinite charm. After the Three Gorges Dam reserved water, "a smooth lake rises in high gorges", it brings up many beautiful landscapes, which endow the new Three Gorges with unique charm. The beauty of the Three Gorges, which contains abundant culture and captures our hearts, will forever be worthy of our seeking again and again. What on earth is the charm of the new Three Gorges? Let us enter the new Three Gorges, a new world together!

Majestätische neue Drei Schluchten

Sanxia-Schluchten des Changjiang-Flußes sind eine große Strecke von Changjiang-Fluß, die stattlichst, herrlich, wunderbar tief und still ist, und gehört zu den Zehn Großen Sehenswürdigkeiten in China. Sie geht westlich von Baidicheng in Kreisstadt Fengjie von Chongqing aus und beendet sich an Nanjing-Paß zu Stadt Yichang der Privonz Hubei. Sie hat eine gesamte Länge von 200 km und besteht aus drei Schluchten wie Qutang-Schlucht, Hexenschlucht und Xilingxia-Schlucht, die zusammen als "Sanxia-Schlucht des Changjiang-Flußes" genannt wurden.

Sanxia-Schlucht des Changjiang-Flußes ist eine konzentrierte Landschaftsgalerie und ein Korridor der Zivilisation an der touristischen Reiselinie für Landsachaft von Changjiang. Sie besitzt eine grenzlose Anziehungskraft und ist ein Meisterwerk der Natur. Wie eine gandiose Syphonie haben die Drei Schluchten des Changjiang -Fluß getrennt ihre eingene Melodien und Anmut. Mit den majestätischen Ufern, steilen Felswünden geht die Qutang-Schlucht ihren Weg, und mit ihrer Tiefe, Stattlichkeit und dem ansteigenden Wolcken sowie Nebel hat die Hexenschlucht charmantes Antreten, aber durch gefährliche Untiefe und seltsame Gebiergkämme, sausendes Wasser entwickelt die Xilingxia-Schlucht ihren eigenen Stil. Zwischen den Schluchten bestehen noch drei Tälern mit breiten Ufern. Wenn man die Ferne umschaut, ist zu sehen, "offenes Land entdehnt sich im Dunst von Vier Seiten, Haushalte teilen sich in halber Höhe des Berges". Man kann gleich einen Gefühl haben, ob er eine flammende Musik hört und ein wunderbarer tiefer Klang dringt in seinen Herz ein. Die Drei Schluchten des Changjiang-Flußes wurden in allen Zeiten immer von den Dichtern und Schriftstellern gepreist und gerühmt.

Von Zeit der Streitenden Reiche, wann der Schriftsteller Qu-Yuan seinen Werk "Lobgesang für Orange" geschrieben hatte, bis zu der Zeit der Südlichen und Nördlichen Dynastie, wann Li Daoyuan sein Werk "Shuizhujing . Flußwasser" geschrieben hatte, haben sich die Drei Schluchten des Changjiang-Flußes dazwischen nicht geändert; und von Zeit der Tang-Dynastie, wann der Dichter Li Bai sein Gedicht "Abgehen in Frühe von Baidi-Stadt" bis zu der Zeit der Song-Dynastie, wann der Dichter Lu You sein Werk "Erzählung über Eintreten in Sichuan" geschrieben hatte, haben die Drei Schluchten des Changjiang-Flußes dazwischen keine Änderung vorgenommen; und weiter bis zu Zeit der Ming- und Qing-Dynastie, wann der englische Lide sein Werk "mit flachen Boot durch Sanxia-Schluchten" geschrieben hatte, haben sich die Drei Schluchtendes Changjiang-Flußes dazwischen auch nicht geändert, geändert sind nur, daß die Zahl der Affen immer reduziert und der Waldumfang immer verkleinert wurde.. Anfang der Gründung der VR CH hat die Regulierung der Drei Schluchten mit der Zersprengung des großen Yanyu-Riffs an Qutang-Schlucht zum Vorspiel begonnen. Manche gefährliche Untiefe waren allmählich verschwunden. In den 80ger Jahre des 20. Jahrhunderts hat die Drei Schluchten des Changjiang-Flußes von altes her eine Änderung zu See durch Verwirklichung der ersten Eindämmung des Flußes bei der Gezhouba-Anlage vorgenommen.

Am 1. Juni 2003 wurde die weltbekante Sanxia-Anlage des Changjiang-Flußes mit der Wasserspeicherung begonnen. Und nach kurzen 10 Tagen sind die großen Veränderungen in der Welt vor sich gegangen. Die Wasserspeicherung erreicht schon die Höhe von 135m über dem Meerspiegel. Und vier Monaten danach ist der Wasserstand an die Höhe von 139m gestiegen, so daß die ganze Region von Drei Schluchtendes Changjiang-Flußes eine gründliche Veränderung vorgenommen hat. Die Drei Schluchten sind ein riesiger künstlicher See gewandelt worden. Als ein Fluß haben die Drei Schluchtendes Changjiang-Flußes ihr originales Aussehen nicht mehr. Der mehr als 01.Mrd. Jahre nach Osten fliessende Fluß hat seinen Schritt verlangsamt. Das Wasser fließt ruhig und sanft, der trübes und gelbe Wasser verwandelt sich allmählich in Dunkelgrün und spiegelt zum erstmal die Berge. Was vergangen soll, ist vergangen, was neut geboren werden soll, ist geboren. Die neue Saxia-Schlucht ist zur Welt gekommen!

Das Sanxia-Projekt war ein Traum der Chinesen seit einem Jahrhundert. Aber als heute dieser Traum verwirklicht wurde, wird unsere alte und schöne Heimat bei uns ein vergangener Traum sein. Ja man kann nicht alles haben! Gegenüber den heutigen Hoch-Schluchten und dem flachen See haben wir einen komplizierten Gefühl von ausreichender Heiterkeit und Erleichterung. Die Sanxia-Schluchthaben zwar keine Schönheiten von Seltsamkeit, Gefährlichkeit, Ruhigkeit und Untiefe mehr, aber sie haben die neuen Schönheiten von Unübersehbarkeit und weiterer Erstreckung. Wichtig ist, daß genau die Sanxia-Anlage gebaut wurde, so daß die moderne Neustadten entstehen , die sich zahlreich wie Sterne in der Zone von Sanxia-Stausee verteilen und die Menschen von Sanxia mindest um eine Halbe des Jahrhunderts vorfrlislig ins Leben der modornen Monschen eintreten können!

Stattliche neue Sanxia-Schlucht ist voller von Anziehungskraft! Nach der Wasserspeicherung von Sanxia-Stausee werden mehre stattliche Sehenswürdigkeiten durch die Hochschluchten und den Flachsee geschafft und wird die Natur mit schönen Bergen und Wasser gebildet. Die Schönheit von Sanxia-Schlucht enthält die Kultur und erobert unsren Herz. Sie ist würdig, daß wir einmal übers anderes danach suchen, was für eine Anmut die neuen Sanxia-Schlucht hat. Lassen wir zusammen in die Sanxia-Schluchten, in eine neue Welt eintreten!

1

1 三峡航拍
1 A Photo of the Three Gorges
Shot in the Air
1 Drei Schluchten aus
Luftphotographie

2 層林盡染
2 All Woods far near resembling
to be dyed in red
2 Gefärbte Wälder in mehren
Schichten

3 滿山紅葉似彩霞（ 巫峽 ）
3 Red leaves on the mountain resembling rosy clouds(Wu Gorge)
3 Rotblätter vom ganzen Berg sind farbigen Wolken ähnlich (Hexenschlucht)

4 西陵春色
4 Xiling Gorge in Spring
4 Frühling in Westgrabschlucht

5

5 截斷巫山雲雨──三峽工程遠眺
5 Holding back the Clouds and Rain of the Wu Mountain (A Distant View of the Three Gorges)
5 Wolken und Regen von Hexenberg unterbrechen— von weiter über das Drei-Schluchten-Projekt blicken

重慶市

　　山是一座城，城是一座山，美麗的重慶市位于中國的西南部，地處長江上游，是中國最年輕的直轄市，也是中國行政轄區面積最大和人口最多的直轄市，現轄40個區縣市，總人口近3100萬，重慶市中心城區渝洲半島被浩瀚的長江和秀麗的嘉陵江擁抱。重慶依山傍水，錯落有致，千姿百態，以"山城"和"霧都"而聞名海內外。

　　重慶是一座已有三千多年的歷史文化名城，200萬年前的巫山人化石，表明重慶地區是人類文明的發祥地之一，半個多世紀，特別是近二十年來，重慶日新月异，已發展成爲中國西部最大的工商業城市和長江上游最重要的物資集散地，成爲追趕世界經濟浪潮的國際大都市。

　　重慶的旅游資源極爲豐富，是我國著名的旅游城市，是三峽庫區旅游綫上重要的組成部分，其景觀以峽穀山水風光爲代表，集山、水、林、泉、瀑、峽、洞于一體，融巴人文化、民族文化、三峽文化、抗戰文化和都市文化于一爐，走進重慶，你會感受到她真像嵌在祖國大地美麗的浮雕。燈的城市、燈的大江；綠的山野、綠的江流，分外妖嬈。

Chongqing

Located in Southwest China on the upper reaches of the Yangtze River, Chongqing is the youngest municipality directly under the central government and the largest municipality in China in terms of administrative area and population. Currently, Chongqing is composed of 40 districts and counties with a total population of approximately 31,000,000. Yuzhou Peninsula, central urban area of Chongqing, is embraced by the grand Yangtze River and the beautiful Jialing River. Chongqing is surrounded by mountains and rivers, and exhibits a diversity of breathtaking sceneries, thus known around the world as "Mountain City" and "Foggy City".

With a history of over 3000 years, Chongqing is a famous city with extensive historical and cultural heritage. 2,000,000-year-old fossil of Wushan Man indicates Chongqing region as one of the cradles for human civilization. In the past five decades, particularly in the recent twenty years, Chongqing has witnessed a rapid growth and become the largest industrial and commercial city in West China and the most important distribution center on the upper reaches of the Yangtze River as well as an international metropolis geared up with the world's economic trend.

Endowed with sufficient tourist resources, Chongqing is also a famous tourist city in China. As an integral part of the Three Gorges Reservoir tourist route, Chongqing exhibits a fascinating landscape typical of mountain and water views. Composed of mountains, rivers, forests, springs, waterfalls, gorges and caves, and integrated with Ba People culture, national culture, Three Gorges culture, Anti-Japanese War culture and urban culture, Chongqing looks like an exquisite relief embedded in the vast land of China. Lantern-decorated avenues and rivers as well as green mountains and rivers make Chongqing all the more fascinating.

6 重慶市人民大禮堂
6 Chongqing People's Auditorium
6 Volksfesthalle der Stadt Changqing

7 大禮堂牌坊
7 Memorial Gateway of the Auditorium
7 Gedenkbogen von Grosser Festhalle

8

9

Stadt Chongqing

Berg ist Stadt, Stadt ist Berg. Die schöne Stadt Chongqing befindet sich im Südwesten von China, und liegt auf dem Oberlauf des Changjiang-Flußes. Sie ist die jüngste regierungsunmittelbare Stadt, die mit dem Verwaltungsgebiet und Bevölkerung an erster Stelle in China steht. Unter deren Verwaltung stehen 40 Bezirke, Kreise, und Städte. Sie hat eine gesamte Befölkerung von 31Mio.Einwohner. In Chongqings Stadtzentrum umarmen der unermäßliche Changjiang-Fluß und zierliche Jialing-Fluß die Yuzhou-Halbinsel. Changqing steht am Fuß des Bergs und dicht bei dem Fluß und verstreut deren Naturgestalungen überallhin. Sie ist als "Bergstadt" und "Nebelstadt" in der Welt bekannt.

Chongqing ist eine alte berühmte Kulturstadt mit einer Geschichte von mehr als 3000Jahren. Die Fossillien von Hexenberg-Menschen aus Zeit vor 2Mio. Jahren zeigen darauf, daß die Gegend von Chongqing einer der Ursprungsorte der Zivilisation der Menschheit. Seit mehr als halbem Jahrhundert, insbesondere seit letzten zwanzig Jahren hat sich die Stadt Chongqing von Tag zu Tag geändert und sich zu der größten industriellen Stadt mit Haldelsverkehr in Westen Chinas und zu einem wichtigen Sammel-und Verteilungszentrum der Materialien auf dem Oberlauf des Changjiang-Flußes entwickelt. Heute ist sie eine internationale Metropole zur Nacheiferung in wirtschaftlicher Strömung geworden.

Chongqong hat sehr reiches touristisches Ressourcen und ist eine berühmte touristische Stadt in China und auch ein wichtiger Bestandteil der Reiselinie von Drei Schluchten-Stauseegebiet. Mit Landschaft von Drei Schluchten als Vertretung wurden die Berge, Wasser, Wälder, Quelle, Wasserfälle, Schluchten und Höhle integriert und die Kultur von Ba-Menschen, Nationale Kultur, Kultur von Drei Schluchten, Kultur von Widerstandkrieg gegen Aggression und Kultur der Metropole in einen Topf geworfen. Wenn man in Chongqing eintritt, wird er den Gefühl haben, daß sie einem auf dem großen Land Chinas eingelegtes schönen Reliefbild. geleicht. wie schön ist die Szene, dass die Stadt unter Lampen, Fluß unter Lampen; Berg in Grüne, Wasserstöme in Grüne sind.

8　歌樂山烈士陵園
8　Sculpture of Revolutionary Martyrs at the Cemetery
8　Mausoleum für gefallenen auf dem Gele-Berg

9　朝天門碼頭
9　A dock at chaotianmen
9　Kai von dem Tor zum Himmel

10　山城夜景
10　The Mountain City at night
10　Nachtszenerie der Bergstadt

10

大足石刻

大足石刻是重慶大足縣境內的北山和寶頂山摩崖造像石窟藝術的總稱，1999年被聯合國教科文組織列爲世界文化遺產總錄，是國家重點文物保護單位和國家"AAAA"級旅游景區。大足石刻始建于唐永徽元年（650），歷經五代，盛于兩宋，余續延至明、清，是中國晚期石窟藝術的代表作品。現公布爲文物保護單位的摩崖造像多達75處，雕像5萬余軀，銘文10萬余字。

Dazu Stone Carvings

Dazu Stone Carvings is a general name for grotto arts of bas-reliefs on precipices on North Hill and Baoding Hill in Dazu County, Chongqing. Listed in the general record of the world's cultural heritage by UNESCO in 1999, Dazu Stone Carvings is now a key historical relic preservation unit and a national-level "AAAA" tourist spot in China. As representative works of late grotto arts in China, its construction started in the first year (AD 650) of Yonghui Emperor in Tang Dynasty, lasted through Five Dynasties, got well underway during the period of South and North Dynasties and the remaining part was completed in Ming and Qing Dynasties. What has now been listed as historical relic preservation units includes 75 bas-reliefs on precipices, more than 50,000 statues and over 100,000 characters of inscriptions.

Steineschnitzerei von Dazu

Steinschnitzerei von Dazu ist die Gesamtbenennung von Grottenkunst von Moya-Gestaltungen auf dem Baoding-Berg und Nord-Berg in Gegend des Kreises Dazu zu Chongqing. Diese Steinschnitzerei wurde 1999 von UNESCO in den Hauptkatalog der Kulturerbe der aufgenommen. Sie ist auch ein Kulturgegestand zum Schwerpunktschutz Chinas und touristische Landschaftszone der Klesse "AAAA". Die Steinschnitzerei von Dazu wurde ursrünglich im ersten Jahr von Yonghui der Tang-Dynastie (650) gebaut, und hatte die Fünf Dynastien durchgelaufen und in zwei Song-Dynastien geblüht. Sie hat die Ming-und Qing-Tynastien erlebt und ist das repräsendative Werk von Grottenkunst der Spätzeit Chinas. Hier wurden 75 Moya-Gestaltungen und 50,000 Statuen und Inschriften von 100,000 Schriftzeichen als Kulturgegenstäden veröffentlicht.

13

12

11 大足睡佛
11 Lying Buddha in Dazu
11 Schlafender Budda von Dazu

12 大足千手觀音
12 Thousand Hand Kuan Yin
12 Guanyin-Budda mit tausend Händen

13 石刻造像
13 Stone-carved Statues
13 Gestaltenin Steinschnitzerei

涪陵白鶴梁

　　白鶴梁位于重慶市涪陵區城北長江江中一塊長約1600米、寬約16米的天然巨型石梁。白鶴梁上的石魚石刻，有着重要的科研和史料價值，又有獨特的藝術價值，它既是長江枯水位的歷史記錄，又有"石魚出水兆豐年"和"年年有余（魚）"之意，因此，古人在白鶴梁上刻有"枯水季節，若石魚出水面，則兆年豐千年如許"的石刻題記。

　　白鶴梁上刻有自唐廣德元年（763年）至當代的石刻題記共計164段和石魚圖14尾。在三峽庫區裏與白鶴梁水文石刻齊名的還有豐都的龍床石、雲陽縣龍脊石等，隨着三峽工程下閘蓄水，這些著名的水文石刻已永存江底。

White Crane Beam in Fuling

　　White Crane Beam is a 1600m-long and 16m-wide natural stone beam in the Yangtze River north to Fuling District, Chongqing. Endowed with stone fish carvings, White Crane Beam is of great value as historical records for scientific research as well as unique artistic value. It serves as historical record for dry seasons in the Yangtze River and represents the meaning of "Stone fish predicts a harvest year". Therefore, ancient people carved stone inscriptions "If stone fish gets out of water in dry seasons, it predicts a harvest year" on White Crane Beam.

　　White Crane Beam contains 164 stone inscriptions and 14 stone fish diagrams carved from the first year of Guangde Emperor (AD 763) in Tang Dynasty to modern times. Other aquatic stone carvings in the Three Gorges Reservoir region as famous as White Crane Beam include Dragon Bed Stone in Fengdu and Dragon Spine Stone in Yunyang County. With water storage for the Three Gorges Project, these prestigious aquatic stone carvings will stay underwater forever.

Weißkranich-Balkon

　　Weißkranich-Balkon befindet sich im Norden des Bezierkes Fuling der Stadt Chongqing. Der ist ein Steinbalkon im Changjiang-Fluß mit einer Länge von 1600m und Breite von 16m. Der auf dem Balkon geschnitzte Fisch ist wissenschaftliche Forschung und historische Materialien wert und hat auch den besonderen Kunstwert. Er ist nicht nur die historische Aufzeichnung von Niedrigwasser der Changjiang-Flußes, und als auch hat er die Bedeutung von "Fisch aus dem Wasser verspricht gute Ernte" und "Lebensmittel jähelich überschüßig (Yu gleicher Klang mit Fisch)", deshalb die Leute im Altertum hatte auf dem Balkon die Inschriften "in Niederwasserzeit, wenn sich der Fisch aus dem Wasser zeigt, verspricht es gute Ernte. Es passierte seit tausend Jahren wie so"

　　Auf dem Weißkranich-Balkon wurden seit dem ersten Jahr von Guangde der Tang-Dynastie (763) bis zu heute insgesamt 164 Texte und 14 Fische geschnitzt. Im Stauseegebiet von Drei Schluchten bestehen noch die Steine wie Drachenbettstein im Kreis Fengdu und Drachenrückenstein im Kreis Yuyang, die eben so berühmt wie hydrologische Inschriften an Weißkranichbalkon sind. Nach der Wasserspeicherung in Sanxia-Stausee sind solche berühmten hydrologische Inschriften in den Fluß versunken.

▓ 豐都鬼城

鬼城名山位于重慶豐都縣長江的北岸，與南岸新縣城隔江相望，是我國最大的鬼文化景區，集儒、釋、道、佛爲一體的民俗文化"懲惡揚善"這一主題，使她成爲中國的神曲之鄉，現爲國家"AAAA"級旅游景區，是三峽庫區一個重要的風景區。

據歷史記載和民間所傳：漢代王方平、陰長生二道士曾于平都山修道成仙，后人附會 "陰、王"爲"陰王"，平都山也漸漸附會成"陰曹地府"。鬼城名山古刹多達27座，歷代藝術家在這裏塑造出一座龐大的鬼的國都，主要景點有奈何橋、鬼門關和天子殿等。

▓ Fengdu Ghost Town

Located on the north bank of the Yangtze River in Fengdu County, Chongqing, and opposite to the new town across the river, Fengdu Ghost Town is the largest scenic spot of ghost culture in China, representing the theme of "Punishing the Evil and Awarding the Good" folk culture integrated with Confucius, Sakyamuni, Taoism and Buddhism. As an important scenic spot in the Three Gorges Reservoir region, Fengdu Ghost Town is a national-level "AAAA" tourist spot.

According to historical records and folk legend, Yin Changsheng and Wang Fangping, two Taoist priests in Han Dynasty, practiced religious doctrines on Pingdu Mountain and became gods. Later generations took them as "Yin Wang" (king in the nether world) and gradually, Pingdu Mountain got the name of the "Nether World". Ghost Town comprises 27 ancient monasteries and artists of various dynasties created an enormous town for ghosts. Key scenic spots include Nether Bridge, Gate of the Hell and King's Palace.

▓ Geisterstadt von Fengdu

Die Geisterstadt befindet sich im Kreis Fengdu von Chongqing an der Nordufer des Changjiang-Flußes und steht der Neukreisstadt an der Südufer gegenüber. Sie ist das größte Landschaftsgebiet mit Geisterkultur unseres Landes. Das Tehma "Übeles bestrafen und Wohltat loben" der volkstümischen Kultur, die das Konfuzianismus, Sakyamuni, Taoismus und Buddismus integriet, hat diese Geisterstadt zu der Heimat der heiligen Melodie in China gemacht. Heute ist sie ein touristisches Landschaftsgebiet der Klasse "AAAA" und auch ein wichtige Sehenswürdigkeit von Stauseezone der Drei Schluchten.

Den historischen Aufzeichnungen und dem Sagen nach: In der Han-Tynastie suchten sich zwei taoistische Möchen Wang Fangping und Yin Changsheng nach den Doktrinen vervollkommen und sein beide später Unsterblicher geworden. Ihre Nachkommen stellten die falsche Zusammenhänge von "Yin, Wang" als "Yinwang" (König der Unterwelt) her und sei es allmälich als "Unterwelt oder Jinseits" mißverstanden. In der Geisterstadt bestehen mehr als 27 altertümische Möchskloster und die Künstler aller Dynastien haben hier die Hauptstadt der Unterwelt gestaltet. Die hauptsächliche hier sind die Naihe-Höhlenbrücke, Höhlenport und Palast von Himmelssohn usw.

忠縣石寶寨

　　石寶寨位于重慶忠縣境内長江北岸邊，此寨始建于明萬歷年間，豈今已有300多年歷史，塔樓共12層，通高56米，建于一座陡壁孤峰拔起的巨石上，此石如玉印，又名"玉印山"，相傳爲女媧補天所遺落的一塊鎮妖五彩石。明末譚宏起義，據此爲寨，"石寶寨"名由此而來。石寶寨是我國古建築藝術中的一顆明珠，列爲世界八大奇异建築之一，爲國家重點文物保護單位和國家"AAAA"級旅游景區。

Shibao Fortress in Zhongxian County

　　Located on the north bank of the Yangtze River in Zhongxian County, Chongqing, Shibao Fortress was built over 300 years ago during the reign of Wanli Emperor in Ming Dynasty. Composed of 12 stories, the tower is 56m in full height and located on a soaring-up giant boulder known as "Privy Seal" or "Privy Seal Mountain". As legend goes, Privy Seal is a colored evil-repressing stone left over by Goddess Nuwa when patching the heaven. At the end of the Ming Dynasty, Tan Hong rose up and occupied the mountain as his fortress, hence the name "Shibao Fortress". Shibao Fortress is a bright pearl in China's ancient architectural art and listed as one of the eight marvelous buildings in the world. Now it is a key historical relic preservation unit and national-level "AAAA" tourist spot.

Shibao- Pfahlwerk (Bergfeste) von Zhong-Kreis

　　Das Shibao-Pfahlwerk von Zhongxian-Kreis befindet sich an der Nordufer des Changjiang-Flußes im Gebiet des Zhong –Kreises. Dieses Werk wurde ursprünglich im Jahre Wanli der Ming-Dynastie gebaut und hat eine Geschichte bis heute von 300 Jahren. Es hat 12 Etagen mit einer gesamten Höhe von 56m. Sie liegt auf einem emporragenden riesigen Stein, der wie ein Jadesiegel aussieht, so wurde der Stein "Jadesiegelberg" genannt. Dem Legend nach sei dieser Stein ein Stein zu Unterdrückung von Hexen, den die Fee Nüwo bei der Himmelausbesserung als ein fünffarbigen Stein auf der Erde vergessen hätte. Ende der Ming-Dynastie brucht der Tanghong-Aufstand aus und die aufständliche Armee machte hier zu einer Bergfeste. Daher war der Name "Shibao-Pfahlwerk" (Steinschatz- Bergfeste) aus der Welt gekommen. Das Shibao-Pfahlwerk ist eine Perle der chinesischen Archtektur im Altertum und wurde zu den Acht Seltsamen Erbauten der Welt eingeordnet. Zugleich ist es auch der Kulturgengenständ zum Schwerpungschtz und die touristische Sehenswürdigkeit der Klasse "AAAA" unseses Landes.

23 石寶寨
23 Shibao Fortress
23 Shibao- Pfahlwerk

24 寨門
24 Gate of the stockade
24 Pfahlpforte

■ 雲陽張飛廟

張飛廟位于重慶雲陽縣長江南岸的飛鳳山麓，與雲陽新縣城隔江相望，爲祭祀三國蜀漢名將張飛而建，張飛廟由一組匠心獨遠的古建築組成，氣勢宏偉壯麗。主要建築有正殿、旁殿、結義樓、望雲軒、助風閣、杜鵑亭和得月亭等7座。前5個建築爲紀念張飛而建，后2個建築爲紀念唐代詩人杜甫在此客居兩年而建，是一座難得的文武合廟。

2003年7月，張飛廟已整體搬遷到上游十多公裏的長江邊，新張飛廟不僅保存了原廟的一磚一瓦，所選地形環境與原廟一致，還新增了文物展覽的面積，整體效果更佳。

■ Zhang Fei Temple in Yunyang

Located on the south bank of the Yangtze River at the foot of Feifeng Mountain in Yunyang County, Chongqing, and opposite to the new county town across the river, Zhang Fei Temple was built in memory of Zhang Fei, a famous general in Shu Kingdom during the Three Kingdoms period (220-265), comprising a complex of unique ancient buildings and exhibiting a majestic air. The temple consists of 7 key buildings, including Front Palace, Side Palace, Sworn Brothers Building, Cloud-view Pavilion, Zhufeng Pavilion, Cuckoo Pavilion and Moon Pavilion. The first five buildings were built in memory of Zhang Fei and the last two buildings were built in memory of Du Fu (712-770), a famous poet in Tang Dynasty, who stayed there for two years. Actually, this temple is a unique temple in memory of both civil and martial figures.

In July 2003, Zhang Fei Temple was entirely relocated on the bank of the Yangtze River over 10km upstream. New Zhang Fei Temple inherits every tile and brick from the old temple, and is identical to the old one in terrain and environment. In addition, the new temple has larger space to display cultural relics and can achieve better overall effect.

■ Zhang-Fei-Tempel

Zhang-Fei-Tempel befindet sich am Fuß des Berges von fliegendem Phönix an der Südufer des Changjiangflußes in Gebiet von Kreis Yunyang zu Chongqing und steht der Neukreisstadt von Yunyang an anderer Ufer gegenüber. Er wurde zum Opfern an Zhangfei, der berühmte General vom Shu-und Han-Reich in der Zeit der Drei Reichen, gebaut. Der aus einer Gruppe von künstlerischen und altertümischen Gebäuden bestehende Tempel ist majestätisch und stattlich. Die Haupterbauten sind Haupthalle, Nebenhalle, Bruderschaftsschließungspavillon, Gartenhäuschen zu Blicken der Wolken, Pavillon zur Windhilfe, Pavillon von Kuckkuck und Pavillon zum Genießen des Mondlichts. Die vorderen fünf wurden zum Gedenken an Zhangfei und die hinteren zwei an Dichter Du Fu aus der Tang-Dynastie, der hier zwei Jahre als Gast gewohnt hatte, gebaut. Dieser Tempel ist ein seltener Tempel mit einer Integration von Zivilisation und Militär.

Im Juli 2003 wurde der Tempel im ganze in einen Ort am Fluß, der ca 10 km weiter von Oberlauf des Changjiang-Flußes umgezogen. Bei dem neuen Zhang-Fei-Tempel wurden nicht nur alle Sachen wie Ziegel oder Dachziegel von dem originalen Tempel gehalten, sondern ist die geographische Lage auch mit der originalen übereinstimmt, sowie wurde die Ausstellungsfläche für Archäologie neu geschaftt. Die Gesamteffizenz des Tempels ist noch besser.

25　助風閣
25　Zhufengge, a two-storied pavilion
25　Pavillon von Windhilfe

26　張飛廟内景
26　Inside Zhang Fei Temple
26　Innenbild von Zhangfei-Tempel

27　張飛廟山門
27　Gate of the Memorial Temple
27　Bergpforte von Zhangfei-Tempel

28　張飛廟遠景
28　Vista from Zhang Fei Temple
28　Perspektiv von Zhangfei-Tempel

白帝城

白帝城位于瞿塘峽西口北岸的白帝山頂，一幢幢飛檐樓閣和紅墻碧瓦，掩映在一片郁郁蔥蔥的綠樹叢中，唐代大詩人李白的千古絕句："朝辭白帝彩雲間，千裏江陵一日還，兩岸猿聲啼不住，輕舟已過萬重山。"使白帝城名揚天下，因此，它是三峽著名的游覽勝地。

據史料記載 西漢末年公孫述據蜀稱王，在山上築城，因城中一井常冒白氣，宛如白龍，他便借此自號白帝，并命名此城爲白帝城。公孫述死后，當地人在山上建廟立公孫述人像，稱白帝廟。

白帝廟內有明良殿、武侯祠和觀星亭等明清建築，左右兩側的東西碑林藏有歷代石碑七十四塊，白帝廟前殿內的大型彩塑"劉備托孤"令人蕩氣回腸，讀過《三國演義》的人，都知道"劉備托孤"的故事，這"托孤"之地就是白帝城，公元222年，劉備率20萬大軍東下，爲關羽報仇，遭東吳大將陸遜火攻連營八百裏，敗至巫山建平，劉備終因積勞成疾，臨終前，召丞相諸葛亮于榻前，將長子劉禪、次子劉永、三子劉理托付給諸葛亮，史稱"劉備托孤"。置身于白帝城，仿佛淌洋于歷史的長河之中。

三峽工程蓄水139米水位對白帝城沒有絲毫影響，現在的白帝城三面環水，一面傍山。這座2000年前曾經上演過劉備托孤三國歷史大劇的白帝城，今天已經變成了一座美麗的半島，隨着三峽工程2006年再度蓄水，這裏最終將變成一座蓬萊式的仙島。

Badi Town (White King Town)

Baidi Town is situated on the top of Baidi Mountain on the north bank of the west mouth of the Qutang Gorge. The buildings with red walls and green tiles are half hidden in green and luxuriant trees. It is famous for a poem written by the great poet Li Bai in the Tang Dynasty, "Bidding farewell to Baidi enveloped in colorful clouds, a thousand li return journey is covered in one day. As the monkeys cry ceaselessly on both banks, the light boats speeds past ten thousand peaks." So, it is a famous scenic spot in the Three Gorges.

According historical records, in the late period of the Western Han Dynasty, Gongsun Shu proclaimed himself the king of Shu, the present Sichuan. A well in the town allegedly gave off white steam, shaped like a white dragon. Gongsun Shu declared himself White King, and renamed the town as White King Town. After Gongsun Shu died, local people built a temple on the mountain and made a statue of him in it. This temple was called as the White King Temple.

In the temple are the Mingling Hall, the Wuhou Shrine and the Star-watching Pavilion and other structures built in the Ming and Qing Dynasties. At both sides of the temple are the East and West Tablet Galleries where preserved 74 stone tablets from various dynasties. In the front hall of the White King Temple, there are a group of colorful statues "Liu Bei Entrusting his son". One who read Romance of the Three Kingdoms knows the story of "Liu Bei Entrusting his son", which occurred right in Badi Town. In 222, Lui Bei led 200000 soldiers to the east in order to revenge for Guan Yu, but Liu Bei was defeated, because Lu Xun, a general of the East Wu Kingdom, set fire to the camps of Lui Bei's army. So, Liu retreated to Jianping in Wushan County. Liu Bei was so tired that he fell ill. Before his death, he asked Zhuge Liang, his prime minister, to his bed, and entrusted his second son Liu Yong and third son Liu Li to the care of him. This is the so-called story of "Liu Bei entrusting his son". Now, standing in Baidi town, you seem to be wandering in the long river of history.

The water level of 139 meters of the reservoir didn't affect Baidi Town at all. Now Baidi Town is surrounded by water on three sides and by mountains on the other side. Baidi Town, where the famous historical event of "Liu Bei Entrusting his son"took place in the Three Kingdoms Period 2000 years ago, now has been a beautiful peninsula. With the next water-store of the Three Gorges Project in 2006, it will become a fairy island like Penglai, Shandong Province.

Baidi-Stadt

Die Baidi-Stadt befindet sich an dem Baidi-Berggipfel an Nordfufer der westlichen Flußmündung von Qutang-Schlucht, wo sich die Pavillons mit Dachschwingungen und roten Wänden sowie grünen Dachziegeln unter denüppig gedeihenden und grünen Wald verstecken. Das über tausande Jahre überlieferte Gedicht vom dem großen Dichter der Tang-Dynastie Li

Bai "Ich gehe am Frühmorgen von Baidi-Stadt in farbigen Wolken aus, mit der Farht von tausend Li (500 Kilometer) werde ich in einem Tag in der Stadt Jiangling ankommen. Die Affen von beiden Ufern quieken unaufhörlich, und der leicht Boot ist schon zehn Tausende Berge vorbeigefahren macht die Baidi-Stadt in der Welt bekannt, deshalb ist sie eine bekannte Sehenswürdigkeit von Sanxia-Schluchten.

Nach der historieschen Aufzeichnung: in den letzten Jahren der Westlichen Han-Dynastie machte sich Gongsun Shu gestützt an die Provinz Sichuan zum König und hatte an dem Berg die Stadt gebaut. Da aus einem Brunen steigte der weiße Nebel wie ein weißer Drachen an, so hatte sich der Gongsun Shu unter der Ausnutzung dieser Erscheinung selbst als weißer Kaiser bezeichnet und der Stadt den Name Baidi-Stadt gegeben. Nach dem Tot von Gongsun Shu hatten die Einheimischen an dem Berg einen Tempel gebaut und ein Porträt von Gongsun Shu errichtet. Dieser Tempel wurde als Baidi-Tempel genannt.

Im Baidi-Tempel bestehen die Erbauten aus Ming- und Qing-Dynastien wie Mingliang- Palast, Wuhou-Ahnensaal und Sternebeobachtungspavillon. In der Gedenksteigalerie an beiden Seiten von links und rechts verstecken sich 74 Gedenksteine aus verschiedenen Dynastien. Der große Farbstatue mit Thema "Liu Bei betraut mit einem Waisenkindern" beeindruckt jeden tief. Jeder, der den Roman "Die Drei Reiche" durchgelesen hat, kennt die Geschicht "Liu Bei betraut mit seinen Waisenkindern". Der Ort, wo Liu Bei mit den Waisenkindern vertraut hatte, ist Baidi-Stadt. Im Jahre 222 führte Liu Bei die Armee mit 0.2 Mio. Soldaten nach Osten, um den General Guan Yu zu rächen. Aber die Lius Armee wurde vom dem General des Dongwu-Reiches durch Feuerüberfall besiegt und mußte einen Rückzug bis Jianping zu Hexenberg antreten. Liu Bei war schließlich infolge der Überarbeitung krank geworden. Kurz vor seinem Tot rufte er seinen Kanzler Zhuge-Liang zu ihm und vor seinem Krankenbett vertraut er Zhuge Liang mit seinem ersten Sohn Liu Chan, zweiten Sohn Liu Yong und dritten Sohn Liu Li. Dies wurde in der Historie als "Liu Bei betraut mit seinen Waisenkindern" Genannt. In der Beidi-Stadt kann man einen Gefühl haben, ob er sich im historischen langen Fluß schwingt.

Die Wasserspeicherung bis die Höhe von 139m wird keinesfalls die Baidi-Stadt negativ beeinflußen. Heute ist Baidi-Stadt in drei Seiten von Wasser umgeschloßen und in einer anderer Seite lehnt sie sich an den Berg an. Baidi-Stadt, wo der Held Liu Bei vor 2000 Jahren mit den Waisenkindern vertraut hatte, ist heute eine schöne Halbinsel geworden. Mit weiterer Wasserspeicherung in Sanxia-Anlage vom Jahre 2006 wird hier endlich ein Paladies sein, wo der legendärer Wohnwort der Götter wird.

29 劉備托孤群像
29 Group Statues "Liu Bei Entrusting His sons"
29 Statuengruppe von Lliu Bei vertraut mit seinen Waisenkindern,

30 鳥瞰白帝城
30 A Birds-Eye view of Baidi Town
30 Baidi-Stadt aus Vogelperspektiv

31 觀星亭
31 Star-watching pauilion
31 Sternwarte

■ 瞿塘峽

瞿塘峽是長江三峽的第一峽，雄踞長江三峽的西段，西起重慶市奉節縣的白帝城，東至巫山縣的大溪鎮，全長約 8 公裏，在長江三峽中它雖然是最短的一個峽，卻以其最雄偉險峻而著稱。

長江三峽的西口便是瞿塘峽的夔門，又名瞿塘關，兩岸峭壁對峙，恰似天造地設的大門，南山名"白鹽山"，北山曰"赤甲山"，奔騰咆哮的長江水在經過四川盆地之后，從這裏進入三峽的大門，瞿塘峽內的河寬只有一、二百米，最窄處不過幾十米，兩岸主要山峰可高達 1000 至 1500 米，把滔滔的大江緊束在溝壑之中，船駛峽中，真有"峰與天關接，舟從地窟行"的感覺。唐代著名詩人杜甫曾在這裏欣然吟誦："衆水會涪萬，瞿塘爭一門"。瞿塘峽兩岸陡峭的峽穀，宛如刀斧劈，難怪清代詩人張問陶發出"縱將萬管玲瓏筆，難寫瞿塘兩岸山"的贊嘆，郭沫若過此地也發出了"若言風景，三峽此爲魁"的感慨！

三峽工程蓄水之后，瞿塘峽景點的變化較大，南岸的洞幽泉甘的鳳凰飲水，題刻滿壁的粉壁墻，倒吊和尚等都已被淹沒；北岸的古棧道已大部分被淹而沉入水下，瞿塘峽口著名的灩澦堆礁石已永沉江底，它可是最后一堆見證峽江千百年艱難航運史的礁石。

■ Qutang Gorge

The Qutang Gorge, the first gorge of the Three Gorges, is located in the west part of the Three Gorges. From Baidi Town of Fengjie in Chongqing in the west to Daxi Town of Wushan in the east, its total length is 8 kilometers. The shortest one in the Yangtze Three Gorges, it is the most magnificent and spectacular.

At the west mouth of the Yangtze Three Gorges is Kuimen in the Qutang Gorge, also called as Qutang Pass. Two great mountains stand there face to face straightly, lofty and sharply almost like the gate set by the nature. The south mountain is called as the Baiyan Mountain (the White Salt Mountain). The north one is called as the Chijia Mountain (the Red Coat Mountain). After passing Sichang Basin, the roaring Yangtze River enters the gate of the Three Gorges. In the Qutang Gorge, the width of the river is only one or two hundred meters and the narrowest places are no more than a few dozen meters. The principal mountains on both banks, which are as high as 1000 to 1500 meters, hug the turbulent river in the gorge. When the ship sails in the gorge, you will feel "Peaks towering into the sky, and boats sailing through the hell". Here, the famous poet Du Fu in the Tang Dynasty recited, "All the waters converge at Fu and Wan, fight for the gate at Qutang." Cliffs and bluffs on both banks are sharp enough as if they were just cut by a natural sword. No wonder the poet Zhang Wentao in the Qing Dynasty praised,"Though you have ten thousand clever brushes, it is hard for you to paint the mountains on the both banks of Qutang." Guo Moruo said here, "If you are looking for unusual scenery, Qutang is the best place to visit."

After the Three Gorges stored water, the scenic spots in the Qutang Gorge were changed more. On the south bank, the Phoenix-drinking Spring, the Whitewashed Wall completely covered with carved inscriptions, Monk Hung Upside-down and so on were all submerged. On the north bank, most of the ancient plank roads were under the water too. The famous Yanyudui Rock, the last witness of the sorrow shipping history of thousands of years in the Gorges and River, has sunk into the river forever.

■ Qutang-Schlucht

Qutang-Schlucht ist die erste Schlucht des Changjiang-Fluβes. Sie zeichnet sich als die westliche Strecke der Sanxia-Schlucht des Changjiang-Fluβes ab. Sie geht im westlich von Baidi-Stadt in Kreis Fengjie zu Stadt Chongqing ab, und beendet sich östlich in Gemeinde Daxi zu Kreis Wushan. Mit einer gesamte Länge von 8 km ist sie zwar die kürzeste Schlucht unter den Drei Schluchten, aber sie wurd durch deren majestätischen Ufer, und steilen Felswänden bekannt.

Die westliche Mündung der Sanxia-Schlucht des Changjiang-Fluβes ist der Engpaβ Kuimen von Qutang-Schlucht, da der mit steilen Festwände an beiden Ufern wie ein vom Gott geschaffenes Tor aussieht und deshalb wurde er als Qutang-Paβ genannt. Der südliche Berg heiβt "Weiβsalz-Berg" und nördlicher Berg als "Chijia-Berg". Der Changjiang-Fluβ braust durch Sichuan-Becken und hier ins Tor der Sanxia-Schlucht, hat hier bei Qutang-Schluch eine Breite nur von ein- oder zwei Hunderten Kilometer und die engste Breite nur von einigen Dutzenden Kilometer. Die Hauptberggipfel an beiden Ufern können die Höhe von 1000m oder 1500m erreichen. Der wellende Fluβwasser erscheint, ob der in einer Felsrinne gefesselt wurde. Wenn man mit dem Schiff durch diese Schlucht fährt, wird er den Gefühl haben, daβ der Berggipfel mit dem Himmelstor verbunden ist und der Schiff in der Höhle fährt. Der berühmte Dichter Du Fu aus Tang-Dynastie hatte hier voller Freude gesungen: "Alle Flüsse münden in Fuling und Wan-Kreis zusammen, Qutang-Schlucht strebt nur nach einem Tor". Das Fluβtal mit steilen Felswände an beiden Ufern von Qutang-Schlucht sieht so aus, ob es durch Messer oder Axt gehaut und gehackt. Es ist kein Wunder, daβ der Dichter Zhang Wentao aus Qing-Dynastie die Qutang-Schlucht so gepreist: "Ich kann die wunderbaren Berge an beiden Ufern nicht beschreiben, wenn auch ich zehn tausende hochwertige Pinseln verschreibe. Guo Moruo hatte auch hier seinen Gefühl ausgedrückt: "soll man die seltsamen Sehenswürdigkeiten zählen, muss die Landschaft hier von Sanxia-Schlucht ist an erster Stelle sein".

Nach der Wasserspeicherung in Sanxia-Anlage werden die Sehenswürdigkeiten von Qutang-Schlucht eine groβe Veränderung vornehmen. Viele Sehenswürdigkeiten an Südufer wie Phönix-Quelle aus einer tiefenn Höhle, geputzte Wände voller von geschnitzten Inschriften und der umgekehrt anhängende Möch wurden vom Wasser überschwemmt. Die an der Nordufer liegende Felssteg wurde zum groβen Teil überschwemmt und das bekannte Yanyudui-Riff ist unter dem Wasser gesunken. Dieses Riff ist das letzte, das die Geschicht des Schifftransports über dem Changjiang Fluβ bei Sanxia-Schlucht bezeugt.

32　瞿塘峡鸟瞰
32　A Bird's-Eye View of Qutang Gorge
32　Qutang-Schlucht aus Vogelperspektiv

33 夔門雄姿
33 The Magnificent Kuimen
33 Stattlichkeit von Kui-Men

34

34 風箱峽　　35 粉壁墙石刻
34 Bellows Gorge　　35 The Whitewashed Wall
34 Blasbalgschlucht　　35 Steinschnitzerei an verputzter Wand

大溪文化遺址

長江出了瞿塘峽東口，與南岸的一條名爲大溪的小河匯合，在河口的山間臺地上坐落着重慶市巫山縣大溪鎮，著名的"大溪文化"發掘于此。大溪文化彌補了三峽地區史前文化和浙江的河姆渡文化一樣，也是長江流域重要的人類文化。

Daxi Cultural Relics

Flowing out of the east mouth of the Qutang Gorge, the Yangtze River converges with a small river named Daxi. On a platform land in the mountains at the mouth of the small river is Daxi Town of Wushan County in Chongqing, where the famous Daxi Culture was uncovered. The Daxi Culture filled the blank in prehistorical culture of the Three Gorges region. It is an important culture along the Yangtze River, which is of the same importance as Qujiading Culture in Jingshan County in Hubei Province and Hemudu Culture in Zhejiang Province.

Ruine der Daxi-Kultur

Der Changjiang-Fluß rollt aus der östlichen Mündung bei Qutang-Schlucht und mündet sich mit einem kleinen Fluß namens Daxi an seiner Südufer. Auf einem Gebiet an dieser Mündung liegt die Daxi-Gemeinde zu Wu-Kreis der Stadt Chongqing. Die bekannte "Daxi-Kultur wurd hier ausgegraben. Wie die Hemdu-Kultur in Provinz Zhejiang hat die Daxi-Kultur die vorgeschichtliche Kultur in Region der Sanxia-Schlucht ergänzt, die auch die wichtige Kultur der Menschheit vom Einzugsgebiet des Changjiang-Flußes ist.

36 瞿塘峽秋韵
36 Autunmn Scenery of Qutang Gorge
36 Qutang-Schlucht in Herbst

37 瞿塘峽東口航拍
37 A Photo of the East Mouth of Qutang Gorge Shot in the Air
37 Westmündung von Qutang-Schlucht aus Luftphotographie

37

天 坑

奉節的天坑地縫風景區是喀斯特地貌的極品，一批批中外地質學家和探險家到天坑地縫考察探險後，無不同聲贊嘆爲世界奇觀，是新三峽旅游中一個極爲重要的景區。

世界上最大的小寨天坑位于瞿塘峽東口處的大溪河上游，距奉節縣城66公裏。天坑在地理學上叫岩溶漏門，是溶洞坍陷或地表水流入地下時溶蝕而成。小寨天坑上口直徑622米，下口直徑522米，深666.2米。天坑四面絕壁，如斧劈刀削。天坑裏有山有水，荊棘密布。坑底的暗河從高達數十米的洞中飛奔而出，咆哮奔騰，再從坑底破壁穿石而出，形成了一條美景如畫的迷宮河。

The Heavenly Pit

The Heavenly Pit and Earthly Ditch scenic spot in Fengjie is extremely typical in karst terrain features. After inspecting and exploring there, geologists and adventurers in our country and abroad can't help praising it a marvellous spectacle. It is an extremely important scenic spot of the tour of the new Three Gorges.

The Xiaozai Heavenly Pit, the largest Heavenly Pit in the world, which is 56 kilometers far from Fengjie County, lies on the upper position of the Daxi River at the east mouth of the Qutang Gorge. Heavenly Pit is called as karstic funnel in geology. It formed through collapse of the solution cavity or erosion when the surface water flew into the ground. The diameter of the upper opening of the Xiaozai Heavenly Pit is 622 meters, the lower one 522 meters. It is 666.2 meters deep. On all sides of the Heavenly Pit are steep cliffs, which seems to be cut by an axe. There are mountains, waters and overgrown brambles in the Heavenly Pit. The hidden river on the bottom of the Heavenly Pit runs out of a cave dozens of meters high, rolling and roaring, then goes through cliffs and rocks in the bottom. It is just like a wonderful maze of the river.

Himmelsgrube

Das Landschaftsgebiet von Himmelsgrube und Erdspalte in Fengjie sind die beste Beschaftenheit der Erdoberfläche von Kaste und auch die wichtige Sehenswürdigkeit für Tourismus bei neuen Sanxia-Schluchten. Mehre chinesische oder ausländischen Gruppen aus Geogaphen oder Erforschungsreisenden kammen hier zur Expedition. Und niemand von ihnen lobt diesen Weltwunder nicht.

Xiaozhai-Himmelsgrube, die kleinste Himmelsgrube der Welt ist, befindet sich an dem Oberlan des Daxi-Flußes bei östlicher Mündung der Qutang-Schlucht und entfernt sich von dem Fengjie-Kreisstadt 66km. Die Himmelsgrube heißt

geographisch Karsttrichter, der beim Einsturz der Höhle oder durch Korrosion von Oberflächenwasser, das in die Erde gefloßen war, gebildet werden muss. Der Durchmesser an oberer Öffnung derXiaozhai-Himmelsgrube ist bei 622m, und an unterer Öffnung bei 522m. Diese Himmelsgrube ist 666.2m tief. Alle Wände der I limmelsgrube sind so steil, ob die von Gott mit Axt gehaut würden. In dieser Himmelsgrube bestehen Berg und Wasser sowie dichte Keuschbäumen. Der Untergrundwasserfall braust aus einer Höhle in Höhe von einigen Dotzenden Meter unterhalb von Himmelsgrube und fällt in die kaputte Wand, dann fließt aus den Steinen heraus, wodurch wurde ein Fluß wie im Irrgarten gebildet.

38　天　坑
38　The Heavenly Pit
38　Himmelsgrube

39　天坑絶壁
39　Precipices of the Heavenly Pit
39　Himmelsgrube und steile Felswand

40　巨象探泉
40　Elephant-Tasting Spring
40　Elefant forscht die Quelle

地縫

世界上最長的開井峽地縫位于小寨天坑三四公裏處，全長37公裏，寬1至500余米，深4至900余米，由上游寬轂的原始森林、中游峽轂及消水洞、下游地下河及一綫天構成，呈東北開口的"V"字形。下游的末端有玉梭瀑布、巨象探泉、黑眼、陰陽縫、一綫天等景點。

The Earthly Ditch

3 or 4 kilometers far from the Xiaozai Heavenly Pit, the Kaijin Gorge Earthly Ditch, the longest Earthly Ditch in the world, is 37 kilometers long, 1 to over 500 meters wide and 4 to over 900 meters deep. It includes scenic spots such as primeval forest of broad valleys in the upper position, valleys and the Xiaoshui Cave in the mid-position, underground rivers and the Thread-like Sky in the lower position. It seems to be a letter "V" opening towards the northeast. At the edge of the lower position, the scenic spots are the Jade Shuttle Waterfall, the Elephant-tasting Spring, the Black Eye, the Seam between Human and Nether worlds, the Thread-like Sky and so on.

Erdspalte

Die Kaijingxia-Erdspalte, die längste in der Welt, befindet sich in einem Ort, der sich von Xiaozhai-Himmelsgrube drei oder vier Kilometer entfernt. Sie hat eine Gesamtlänge von 37km, die Breite von 1 bis ca. 500m und die Tiefe von ca. 4 bis 900m. Sie besteht aus dem Breiten Tal mit Urwald an dem Oberlauf, Bergschlucht und Xiaoshui-Höhle an Mittellauf sowie dem Untergrundwasserlan und Himmellichtschimmer an Unterlauf und sieht von Osten nach Westen wie ein "V" Zeichen aus. Am Ende des Unterlanes bstehen die Sehenswürdigkeiten wie Yusu-Wasserfall, Elefant forscht die Quelle, Schwarzloch, Yinyan-Spalte, Himmellichtschimmer usw.

41 俯瞰地縫
41 Overlooking the Earthly Ditch
41 Erdspalte aus Changjiang-Brücke von WestgrabVogelperspektiv

42 地縫之光　　　　　43 黑眼
42 The Earthly Ditch　　43 The Black Eye
42 Licht von Erdspalte　43 Schwarzauge

42

41

43

大寧河小三峽

　　大寧河發源于大巴山南麓的陝西省平利縣，流經重慶的巫溪和巫山兩縣，全長 300 多公裏，在巫峽的西口處注入長江，是長江中最大的一條支流。它從兩千米多高的崇山峻嶺中奔騰而下，切割地表，使得沿途形成了許多峽穀勝景，小三峽是大寧河下游巫山縣境内的一段，它由龍門峽、巴霧峽和滴翠峽組成。這裏無處不蒼翠，有水盡飛泉，船行駛在峽裏，仿佛蕩漾于百裏畫廊之中。

　　三峽工程蓄水之后，現在的小三峽水面上升了許多。龍門峽和巴霧峽的峽穀感已明顯減弱，大型游船能够行駛在波平如鏡的水面上，山巒緩緩地向后隱退，别有一番景象，過去那些險灘和激流早已成爲往日的回憶。今天的小三峽没有了號子，没有了力的張揚，在平穩和恬静中顯得格外温柔。幸虧還有滴翠峽仍然保持着昔日那種險峻的山勢和屹立的峭壁，還能讓我們感覺到小三峽往日的風姿，尤其是滴翠峽中一片片臨水而居的青青翠竹，枝頭垂吊水中，透過竹林觀碧水泛舟，恰是一幅典型的中國山水畫。

　　今天的小三峽依然是那么的秀，它秀得這春水長流一往多情、純得透底、綠得心醉，秀得這綿長的畫廊和閱不盡的人間春色，幽翠入夢，美在長相思。

The Lesser Three Gorges on the Daning River

　　The Daning River originates from Pingli County, Shanxi Province at the southern foot of the Daba Mountain. It passes Wuxi and Wushan counties in Chongqing and flows into the Yangtze River at the west mouth of the Wu Gorge. It is over 300 kilometers long, and it is the biggest tributary in the Three Gorges. Running down from mountains over 2000 meters high, the Daning River cut the earth's surface. So lots of valleys and gorges came into being along the river. The Lesser Three Gorges is the part in Wushan County in the lower position of the Daning River, including the Longmen Gorge, the Bawu Gorge, and the Dicui Gorge. Here everything is green. There are hang waterfalls and flying springs. Sailing in the gorges is like wandering in a long gallery of paintings.

　　After the Three Gorges reserved water, the water level in the Lesser Three Gorges has risen much higher. The gorge sense of the Longmen Gorge and Bawu Gorge weakened obviously. The large-sized pleasure-boat can sail on the smooth river, which looks just a bright mirror. Seeing mountains moving back slowly, you will feel that is a unique view. Now the dangerous shoals and strong currents have been a memory of the past times. Today, with no ballads sang by the boatmen and strength showed by the trackers, the Lesser Three Gorges looks especially gentle and smooth. Luckily, the Dicui Gorge still remains its original appearance with precipitous mountains and steep cliffs in former times, which let us feel the original charisma of the Lesser Three Gorges. Particularly in the Dicui Gorge, there are green bamboos beside the river, dropping their branches to the river. Through the bamboos, to see someone rowing a boat on green water, seems to be appreciating a typical Chinese painting of mountains and waters.

　　Today, the Lesser Three Gorges is still so elegant. The river runs all year around with its deep feelings. It is so clear and pure that you can see the bottom through the water. It is so green that you are intoxicated with it. The long natural gallery and spring scenery in man's world, with full green, come into your dream, let you yearn for it forever.

Kleine Schluchten des Daning-Flußes

　　Daning-Fluß entspringt in Pingli-Kreis der Provinz Shanxi am südlichen Fuß des Daba-Berges. Er fließt durch Wuxi-Kreis und Wushan-Kreis von Chongqing und hat eine Gesamtlänge von mehr als 300km. Er fließt an der westlichen Mündung der Hexenschlucht in den Changjiang-Fluß ein und ist der größte Flußarm von Changjiang. Er braust von dem Gebirge in Höhe von zweitausend Meter herunter schneidet die Erboberfläche, so daß entlang des Flußweges zahlreiche Bergschlucht-Sehenswürdigkeiten gebildet wurden. Die Kleine Drei Schluchten sind eine Strecke von Unterlan des Daning-Flußes in Wushan-Kreis. Sie besteht aus Drachentor-Schlucht, Bawu-Schlucht und Dicui-Schllucht. Hier sind überall mit grüner Bedeckung. Das Wasserende und die fliegene Quelle sind so faszinierend, daß man nicht mehr an Rückkehr denkt. Wenn man mit dem Schiff in der Schlucht fährt, wird einen Gefühl haben, ob er in einer Galerie schwingt.

　　Nach der Wasserspeicherung in Sanxia-Stausee ist der Wasserstand der Kleinen Drei Schluchten viel gestiegen. Bei den heutigen Kleinen Drei Schluchten ist der Gefühl von Schluchten beträchtlich beeinträchtigt. Das große Schiff kann ruhig an dem wellenlosen Wasser fahren, und dabei kann man bewundern, wie sich die Berge oder Hügel langsam zurückziehen und verschwinden. Die gefährliche Untiefe und der reißende Strom sind vergangen und beiben nur als Erinnerung in unserem Herz. Bei den heutign Sanxia-Schluchten haben keine Arbeitslider zu hören und keine herumposaunende Präsentation der Kraft zu sehen. In dieser ruhigen Umgebung erscheinen die Schluchten besonders seanft. Zum Glück hat die Dicui-Schlucht noch deren abschüßige bodenphysikalische Eigenschften, womit können wir noch die vergangene Charme der Kleinen Drei Schluchten fühlen. Besonders sind die Bambushaine zu erwähnen. Die neben dem Wasser stehenden grünen Bambusse strecken deren Zweigspitzen ins Wasser. Wenn man durch diese Bambushaine die Szene von einem Boot über dem Wasser schauen, wird er eine typische chinesische Landschaftsmalerei in Realität haben.

　　Die heutigen Kleinen Drei Schluchten sind immer noch so zierlich, daß der Fluß ihnen aus ganzem Herz und aus ganzer Seele zugetan ist, so rein, daß man sie an den Grund sehen kann , so grün, daß man von ihnen bezaubert wird, und so schön, daß diese lange Galerie und endlose Frühlingsszene in den Traum versenken. Wie schön ist die ewige Liebe.

44　航拍大寧河小三峽
44　The Lesser Three Gorges on the Daning River
44　Kleine Schluchten des Daning-Flußes

44

45 龍門峽
45 Lingmen Gorge
45 Drachentorschlucht

46 巴霧峽
46 Bawu Gorge
46 Bawu-Schlucht

46

47

47 滴翠修竹
47 Green and Slender Bamboos
47 Schlanke Bambusse tropfen grün

48 碧水泛舟
48 Sailing on the green water
48 Bootsfahrt über grünem Wasser

48

大昌古鎮

　　走出滴翠峽，逆流而上幾公裏，游客便能領略到那即將搬遷的巫山縣大昌古鎮最后的風姿，穿過古城的南門，進入大昌古鎮，就如同走進了那悠遠的記憶之中，青石板的小巷裏人很少，從兩邊陳舊斑駁的老房子上還依稀可以看到大昌古鎮往日的繁華，隨着2006年三峽工程再度蓄水，大昌古鎮將變成一個大昌平湖，古鎮1700年的故事和傳說變成爲人們永恒的記憶。

Ancient Dachang Town

　　Coming out of the Dicui Gorge and going several kilometers upstream, travelers can appreciate the last charisma of the ancient Dachang Town, which is about to be migrated. Passing through the south gate of the ancient town, you will seem to enter a distant memory. There are few people on the gray-stone road. From the old mottled houses on both sides, the flourishing in former times of the ancient Dachang Town appears indistinct. When the Three Gorges reserves water again in 2006, the ancient Dachang Town will become Dachang smooth lake. Stories and Legends about the ancient town for 1700 years will be the everlasting memory of people.

Altertümische Dachang-Gemeinde

　　Aus der Dicui-Schlucht fährt man weiter einige Kilomter gegen den Strom. Er wird die letzte Stattlichkeit der altertümischen Dachang-Gemeinde in Kreis Wushan, die gleich umziehen wird. Tritt man durch das Südtor von alter Stadt in die Dachang-Gemeinde ein, geht man in die weitere Erinnerung hinein. An der mit schwarzen Steinplatten belegten Straße der kleinen Gasse sind wenige Leute zu sehen. Von den alten buntscheckigen Häusern kan man noch ersehen, daß die Gemeinde gediehen war. Mit weiterer Wasserspeicherung in Sanxia-Stausee von 2006 wird Dachang-Gemeinde das große Dachang-See werden. Und dabei werden die in 1700 Jahren geschehenen Geschichte und Legende über diese Dachang-Gemeinde auch unsere ewige Erinnerung werden.

49

50

49 古鎮怪柏
49 Grotesque Cypresses in the Ancient Town
49 Seltsame Zypresse in slter Gemeinde

50 古鎮一角
50 A Corner of Ancient Town
50 Eine Ecke der alten Gemeinde

51 古鎮東門
51 The Aast Gate of the Ancient Town
51 Oststadtor von alter Gemeinde

51

巫 峡

巫峡是長江三峡中最爲幽深秀麗的一個峡，西起重慶市巫山縣的大寧河口，東到湖北省巴東縣的官渡口，全長45公裏，它是三峡中既長而又整齊的一峡，所以又叫大峡。巫峡分東西兩段，西段由金盔銀甲峡和箭穿峡組成，東段由鐵棺峡和門扇峡組成。

"瞿塘迎邐盡，巫峡峥嶸起"。長江衝出瞿塘之後，過大寧河寬穀，在重慶巫山縣接訥了大寧河穀，便進入了畫廊般的巫峡。巫峡以幽深秀麗擅奇天下，它峡長穀深，迂回曲折，奇峰綿延，雲霧升騰，景色誘人。 船過巫峡，時而蒼崖相逼，好象江流阻塞，忽而峰回路轉，別有江天。

"放舟下巫峡，心在十二峰。"游覽巫峡，人們最感興趣的恐怕就是巫峡十二峰，尤其是三峡工程蓄水139米之後，人們關心的是巫峡十二峰的風姿是否依舊，"神女應無恙，當今世界殊！" 今天的巫峡十二峰仍競秀爭雄，神女峰依然地俏麗，浪漫動人的神話傳說吸引着無數游客心馳神往。

三峡工程蓄水139米以后，除了巫峡十二峰以外，巫峡裏一些著名的景點和文景觀，如原川鄂邊界的 "楚蜀鴻溝" 題刻。懸崖絕壁上夔巫古棧道，刻在江邊岩石上的縲縲纖痕等，都全部或部分沉入江中。出巫峡東口就是湖北省巴東縣的官渡口鎮，長江從這裏便進入了香溪河寬穀。

Wu Gorge

The Wu Gorge, the second gorge of the Yangtze Three Gorges, is about 45 kilometers long, extending from the mouth of the Daning River in Wushan County of Chongqing in the west, to Guandukou of Badong County, Hubei Province in the east. Because it is a long and neat gorge, it is also called as the Great Gorge. The Wu Gorge is divided into east and west two sections. The west section consists of the Golden Helmet and Silver Armour Gorge and the Arrow-passing Gorge. The east section consists of the Iron Coffin Gorge and the Door Gorge.

"When the Qutang rolls on to an end, the Wu Gorge rises with its lofty peaks." Rushing out of the Qutang Gorge, the Yangtze River passes through the Daning River Broad Valley, takes in the Daning River in Wushan County of Chongqing, then goes into the gallery-like Wu Gorge. The Wu Gorge is noted for its deep and serene. It is long and deep, full of zigzags. There are weird peaks with mists rising. The beautiful sights are fascinating. Traveling through the Wu Gorge in a boat, one sometimes may find the way blocked by mountains. But a sharp turn of the boat brings one to an area of entirely different scenery.

"Sailing downstream to the Wu Gorge, I have my heart only in the Twelve Peaks of the Wu Mountain." When traveling in the Wu Gorge, people are most interested in the Twelve Peaks of the Wu Gorge. Particularly after the water level reached 139 meters, they are most concerned about whether the charisma of the Twelve Peaks of the Wu Gorge still remain, particularly after the water level reached 139 meter. "The Goddess Peak if she is still there, will marvel at a world so changed." Today, the Twelve Peaks still compete their beauty and magnificence each other. The Goddess Peak is still slim and elegant. Romantic stories and legends attract countless tourists.

After the water level rose to 139 meters, except the Twelve Peaks of the Wu Gorge, a few famous scenic spots and cultural relics were completely or incompletely submerged, such as the engraved inscription "the Chasm between Hubei and Sichuan" at the border of the original Sichuan and Hubei, the ancient Kuiwu plank roads on cliffs, deep traces marked by towing on the rocks beside the river. Out of the east mouth of the Wu Gorge is Guandukou Town of Badong County, Hubei Province, where the Yangtze River flows into the Xiangxi River Broad Valley.

Hexenschlucht

Hexenschllucht ist die tiefste und zierlichste von drei Sanxia-Schluchen des Changjiang-Flußes. Sie geht westlich von Daning-Flußmündung im Krei Wushan von Stadt Chongqing aus, und beendet sich in Guandukou. Sie hat eine Gesamtelänge von 45km und wurde auch Großschlucht genannt, weil sie so lang und ordentlich und anständig ist. Sie teilt sich in Oststrecke und Weststrecke. Die Weststrecke bsteht aus dem Tal von Goldppanzer und Silberhelm, Tal von Pfeilerbohrung, und die Oststrecke besteht aus Tal von Eisensarg und Tal von Torflügel.

"Qutang kommt allen Schönheiten entgegen, Hexenschlucht begrüßt steil emporsteigende Berge". Changjiang-Fluß strömt von Qutang aus und fließt durch das Danning-Breittal dann nimmt in Kreis Wushan von Chongqing das Daning-Tal an. Anschließend geht er in die Hexenschlucht, die so schön wie Galerie ist. Hexenschlucht wurde durch ihre Tiefe, Stattlichkeit sowie ansteigende Wolcken und Nebel in der Welt bekannt. Wenn man mit Schiff in Hexenschlucht fährt, wird er erleben, wie die überhängende Klippen von beiden Seiten auf einmal ihn zwingen, ob der Fluß verstopft ist, und wie an anderemal die Berge verschwunden sind und und das Schiff über einem normalen Flußlan fährt.

"Fährt man mit Boot durch Hexenschlucht, bleibt sein Herz bleibt bei Zwölf Bergengipfel". Bei der Besichtigung der Hexenschlucht interessirt man zum meisten für Zwölf Begengipfel. Besonders nachdem die Sanxia-Anlage die Wasserspeicherung bis die Höhe von 139m angenommen hat, interessirt man daran, ob die Zwölf Begengipfel genau wie früh ihre Charme behalten wird. "Geisterfee ist gesund wie zuvor, heutige Welt ist wundbar". Heute streben die Zwöl Berggipfel nach Hegemonie immer noch und Göttingipfel ist so schön wie zuvor. Das romatische Märchen faszinieren zahlreiche Besucher.

Nach der Wasserspeicherung bis die Höhe von 139m in Saxian-Anlage werden außer den Zwöl Berggipfeln alle bekannten Sehenswürdigkeiten wie geschnitzte Inschriften an der Grenze von Provinzen Hubei und Sichuan, alte an Felswand gebaute Holzstege, die tief in Steinen geprägten Treidelspure ganz oder zum Teil in den Fluß versenken. Aus der östlichen Mündung der Hexenschlucht kommt man in die Gemiene Guandukou von Kreis Badong der Provinz Hubei., von hier fließt Changjiang-Fluß ins Duftbach—Breittal.

52

52

52　巫峡航拍
52　A photo of Wu Gorge Shot in the Air
52　Hexenschlucht aus

53

53 神女峰　　54 漫江碧透
53 Goddess Peak　　54 The Full Green Giver
53 Geisterfeegipfel　　54 Fluß grundlich in Grün

54

神农溪

神農溪又名沿渡河，位于巴東新縣城的北岸，是長江走出巫峽進入香溪寬穀之後的第一條支流，發源于我國著名的"華中第一峰"之稱的湖北神農架原始森林主峰的南坡，全長60公裏。千百年來，神農溪像龍一樣雄距于千重大山和萬道深淵之間，最后在湖北巴東境内的西壤口，悄悄地擁入浩瀚的長江懷抱。

三峽工程蓄水之前，游客游覽神農溪要乘坐原始、古樸的土家族"碗豆角"木制扁舟放漂，游客一路上可以盡情地領略優美動人的土家族巴山舞，還有高亢激昂的纖夫號子，令人怦然心動。

三峽工程蓄水之後，游客游覽神農溪要改乘大型環保游船，這種環保船在蓄水前是進不了神農溪的，神農溪的峽穀并沒有因水面升高而使峽穀感减弱，兩岸相距不過五六十米，山峰依然高聳，游船碧波蕩漾，穿行于峽穀之間，忽而向左露出一灣幽穀，忽而向右拐出一片新的天地。

今天的神農溪是一片綠色的世界，水是濃綠的，山是翠綠的，而且是一種伸手可及的綠。這裏已成爲新三峽中一個峽穀幽深、綠樹叢蔭、水清倒影、風景如畫的旅游勝地。

Shennongxi River

The Shennongxi River, also called the Yandu River, is located on the north bank of the new Badong County. It is the first tributary, which the Yangtze River meets after coming out of the Wu Gorge to go into the Xiangxi River Broad Valley. It originates from the south hillside of "the first peak in the middle of China"— the main peak of the Shennongjia Primeval Forest in Hubei. The total length is 60 kilometers. For thousands of years, the Shennongxi River lies among countless mountains and deep valleys like a huge dragon. Then, at Xirongkou in Badong County, Hubei Province, it is holded in the arm of the vast Yangtze River quietly.

Before the Three Gorges reserved water, to visit the Shennongxi River, tourists should raft downstream by taking a primeval pea-like wooden boat. On the way, they can enjoy graceful and moving Bashan Dance of the Tujia Minority and loud and sonorous ballads sang by boat trackers. How interesting and exciting!

After the Three Gorges Project reserved water, tourists can take a kind of large-sized environmental-protection ship, which was not able to enter the Shennongxi River before. The rising of the water level didn't weaken the gorge sense of the gorges of the Shennongxi River. The distance between both banks of the river is only 50 to 60 meters. Mountains are still lofty. When the ship sails on the river and passes through the gorges, sometimes you will find there is a deep gorge on the left, sometimes there appears another world after the ship turns right.

Today, the Shennongxi River is a green world. Waters are green. Mountains are green. And this green is just beside your hand. With deep gorges, flourishing trees and shadows reflecting on clear waters, this place has been a beautiful resort in the new Three Gorges.

Shennong-Bach

Shennong-Bach, auch Yandu-Fluß genannt, befindet sich im Nordteil der neuen Kreisstadt Badong. Er ist der erste Flußarm von Changjiang –Fluß, nachdem Changjiang von Hexenschlucht in das Xiangxi-Breittal eingetreten ist. Shennong-Bach entspringt dem südlichen Bergabhang des berühmten Hauptgipfels "Ersten Gipfel Chinas" von Shennongjia-Urwald in Provinz Hubei. Es hat eine Gesamtlänge von 60 km. Seit mehrtausend Jahren liegt Shennong-Bach wie ein Drachen zwischen den Bergen und tiefen Gebirgestälern. Er mündet schließlich unbemerkt bei Xirangkou in Kreit Badong der Provinz Hubei in den unermeßlichen Changjiang-Fluß.

Vor der Wasserspeicherung in Sanxia-Anlage soll man per urspünglichen und einfachen Flachholzboot (Gebogene Bohnenhülse) von Tujia-Nationatät zur Besichtigung von Shennong-Bach fahren. Unterweg kann man nach Herzenzlust den schöen Bashan-Tanzkunst der Tujiang- Nationalität und die erhabenen Klänge der Arbeitslieder von Treidlern genießen.

55

Nach der Wasserspeicherung in Sanxia-Anlage wird man im Gegenteil per großen umweltfreunlichen Dampfer fahren. Dieser Dampfer kann vor der Wasserspeicherung nicht in den Shennong- hineinfahren. Bei der Schlucht von Shennong-Bach wurde der Schluchtsgefül nicht durch Erhöhung des Wasserstandes beeinträchtigt. Zwischen beiden Ulfer besteht eine Entfernung nur von 50 oder 60m. Die Berggipfel ragen noch empor. Wie schön ist, daß der Dampfer mal durch tiefes Tas fährt, mal nach links in ein anderes Tal einbiegt, und mal nach rechts in eine neue Welt einfährt.

Heute ist Shennong-Bach eine grüne Welt, wo das Wasser in Grün, Berge in Grün, und alles ist die mit Hand berührbare Grüne. Mit den tiefen Tälern, grünen Wädern, klarem Wasser und schöner Landschaft ist hier schon ein Besichtigungsort für Tourismus geworden.

56

56

56

55　鴨子口　　　　56　綿竹峽
55　Yazikou　　　　56　Mianzhu Gorge
55　Entenschnauze　56　Weichbambusschlucht

■ 神农溪

　　與大寧河小三峽一樣，神農溪也分三個峽段，三峽工程畜水后，龍昌洞峽和鸚鵡峽變化較大，棉竹峽還相對原始，旅游部門在這裏開發了船夫裸體拉縴的新項目，以彌補神農溪原始風情消失所帶來的遺憾。從這些船夫們嘴裏引吭高歌的號子聲，貼着石壁，貼着溪流，貼着卵石灘，在峽穀中傳響，神農溪風光很美，人更美，并且這種美是永恒不變的……

■ Shennongxi River

　　As the same as the Daning River on the Lesser Three Gorges, the Shennongxi River consists of three sections. After the Three Gorges Project stored water, the Longchangdong Gorge and the Parrot Gorge were changed most. The Mianzhu Gorge is relatively primeval, where the tour department developed a new item that the naked boatmen tow boats to make up for the regret of the lost primeval feeling. Loud ballads sang by boatmen echo in the gorges, along the cliffs, along the stream, along the stone shoals. The scenery of the Shenongxi River is beautiful, and the people of Shennongxi are more beautiful! The beauty will last forever...

■ Shennong-Bach

　　Genau wie die Kleinen Drei Schluchten des Daning-Flußes teilt sich Shennong-Bach auch in drei Schluchtestrecken. Nach der Wasserspeicherung in Sanxia-Anlage haben sich die Longchang-Schlucht und Papagei-Schlucht viel geändert. Die Mianzhu-Schlucht ist relativ ursprünglicher. Die Gesellschaft für Tourismus hat hier ein neues touristisches Programm bzw. Schiff-Treideln von nackten Treidlern geschaffen, um die bedauerliche Sache, daß der ursprüngliche Antliz und Stil von Shennong-Bach verschwunden wurden, zu bedecken. Der Klang des Arbeitsliedes aus dem Mund der Treidlern hallen entlang der Felswänd, dem Flußchen, Kieselstrand im Tal wieder. Die Landschaft von Shennong-Bach ist schön, aber die Menschen hier sind noch schöner, und diese Schönheit ist evwg und unveränderbar...

57　幽深秀麗的綿竹峽
57　The Deep and Elegant Mianzhu Gorge
57　Tiefe und zierliche Weichbambusschlucht

58 土家族民俗歌舞——巴山舞
58 The folk song and dance of the
Tujia Minority-the Bashan Dance
58 Volkestanz der Tujia -Nationalität
– Baschan-Tanz

■ 屈原祠

屈原祠坐落于古城歸州鎮，這座有2300多年的歷史的城池很小、全城僅有0.6平方公裏，但作爲風雨峽江的滄桑見證，歸州有不可替代的歷史地位，它曾演繹過古夔子國的神秘；楚國的興衰；三國的壯烈；唐朝的飄逸；宋明的清麗；清朝和近代的頹廢與勃興……

屈原祠是爲紀念屈原而修建的，屈原，名平。公元前340年誕生于秭歸縣樂平裏，是我國最早的偉大愛國詩人。他曾在古代楚國做過左徒和三閭大夫，后因奸臣排擠而被放逐江南，當楚國被秦兵攻破時，他憤而以身殉國，投汨羅江而死。其《離騷》、《九章》、《九歌》等詩篇，聲貫古今，名揚中外，1953年，聯合國教科文組織將屈原列爲世界文化名人。

三峽工程的蓄水139米水位后，對長江三峽著名景點湖北秭歸的屈原祠影響不大，現在的屈原祠是1976年因葛洲壩工程的興建由屈原沱搬遷重建，隨着三峽工程的再度蓄水，它作爲"三峽移民"又面臨第二次搬遷，東遷至新縣城茅坪鎮的鳳凰山。

■ Qu Yuan Shrine

The Qu Yuan Shrine is located in the ancient Guizhou Town. Though this town of a 2300-year history is very small, only 0.6 square kilometers, it is of an unchangeable position in history as the witness of the changes in the Gorges and River. Here occurred many important events in the past dynasties, glories or disgraces and prosperous or decline...

The Qu Yuan Shrine was built to memorize Qu Yuan. Qu Yuan, also named Ping, the earliest patriotic poet in China, was born in 340 B.C. in Lepingli of Zigui County. He once served as a supervisor and imperial household administrator in the ancient Chu State. Then, squeezed by malicious minister, he was expelled to a place south of the Yangtze River. When the army of the Qing State captured the Chu, he was so overcome with indignation and sorrow that he jumped into the Miluo River. His poems and articles including Laments at parting, Nine Lyrical Poems and Nine Sacrificial Songs are well known all over the world. In 1953, Qu Yuan is listed to one of the cultural famous men in the world by UNESCO.

After the water level rose to 139 meters, the Qu Yuan Shrine, which is a famous scenic spot of the Three Gorges in Zigui of Hubei, was affected little. The Qu Yuan Shrine was moved from Quyuantuo and rebuilt in 1976 because of the construction of the Gezhouba Dam Project. Because the Three Gorges Project will reserve water again, it has to be removed east to the Phoenix Mountain of Maoping Town in Zigui County.

■ Qu-Yuan-Tempel

Qu-Yuan-Tempel befindet sich in alter Stadt Guizhou der Gemeindenebe. Diese kleine Stadt hat eine 2300 jährige Geschichte. Sie hat zwar eine Bodenfäche nur von 0.6m³. aber als der Zeuger vieler Wechselfälle des Changjiang-Flußes besitzt sie den unersetzbarn Platz in der Geschicht. Sie hatte das Mystizismus des alten Kuizi-Reiches, Gedeihen und Abgang des Chu-Reiches, Heldentum von Drei Reichen, Anmute der Tang-Dynastie, Stattlichkeit der Song-Dynastie, Dekadenz der Qing-Dynastie und Anschwung der Neuzeit deduziert...

Qu-Yaun-Tempel wurde zum Gedenken an Quyaun gebaut. Qu Yuan, namens Ping, geb. im Jahre 340 v.Z in Lepingli der Kreisstadt Zigui, war der früheste große patriotische Dichter Chinas. Im Altertum war er ein Beamter für Verwaltung von drei Gassen des Chu-Reiches. Später wurde er von dem ungetreueren Hochbeamter des Kaisers weggestoßen und an das südliche Gebiet des Changjiang-Flußes verbannt. Als Chu-Reich von seinem Feind Qin-Rech besiegt wurde, hatte er sich in den Miluo-Fluß geworfen und sein Leben für sein Vaterland hingegeben. Seine Gedichte wie "Lisau", "Neun Kapite", "Neun Lieder" usw. überliefern bis heute und sind in der Welt bekannt. 1953 wurde Qu Yuan von UNESCO zu den weltbekannten Literaten gezäht.

Die Wasserspeicherung in Sanxia-Anlage bis Höhe von 139m wird den Qu-Yuan-Tempel, die berühmte Sehenswürdigkeit in Kreis Zigui der Provinz Hubei, nicht viel negativ beeinflußen. Der heutige Qu-Yuan-Tempel ist im Jahre 1976 wegen der Ausführung des Gezhouba-Damms von Qu-Yuan-Bucht hier sumgezogen und umgebaut. Mit der weiteren Wasserspeicherung in Sanxia-Anlage kommt der Tempel dem zweiten Umzug entgengen. Er wird östlich an den Phönix-Berg in Gemeinde Maoping der Neustadt umziehen.

59

60 屈原紀念館
60 Qu Yuan Memorial Hall
60 Gedenkhalle für Qu Yuan

61 屈原墓
61 Qu Yuan's Grave
61 Grab von Qu-Yuan   Gedenksteinegalerie

02 屈原祠山門
62 The Gate of Qu Yuan Shrine
62 Bergtor von Qu –Yuan-Tempel

屈原故裏

　　屈原故裏位于秭歸縣屈原鎮三閭村樂平裏, 從地處西陵峽西段兵書寶劍峽中的北岸屈原鎮出發, 乘車約一小時便可到達樂平裏, 三峽工程175米蓄水后, 游客也可乘船由香溪河賈家店處進入七裏峽, 穿過七裏峽幽穀后, 一片開闊地便是樂平裏。

　　游客一進入樂平裏, 便可看柑橘林中蔟擁着一座莊嚴而亮麗的樂平裏牌坊, 它似乎告訴人們來到了一代偉人的誕生地! 這裏有關屈原的名勝古迹和傳説特別多, 古人曾集爲 "八景", 如屈原廟、照面井、香爐坪和讀書洞等, 其中保存最爲完好的景點當屬屈原廟, 蒼青的樹、逸香的花、古樸的建築、莊嚴的塑像, 營造出屈原建築的特有風格。

Qu Yuan's Hometown

　　Qu Yuan's hometown is situated at Lepingli of Sannu Village in Quyuan Town of Zigui County. Off Quyuan Town on the north bank of the tactics book and sword Gorge in the west section of the Xiling Gorge, about one hour's drive will take you to Lepingli. After the water level reaches 175 meters, you can sail from Jiajiadian in the Xiangxi River to enter the Qili Gorge. After passing through the deep Qili Gorge, you can see an open land°™°™Lepingli.

　　As soon as you get to Lepingli, a solemn memorial archway surrounded by orange trees appears in your eyes, which seems to tell you here comes the native place of a great man. There are so many places of historic interest and scenic beauty and legends about Qu Yuan that they were collected as "Eight Sceneries" such as the Qu Yuan Temple, the Mirroring Well, the Incense Burner level-land and the Book-reading Cave, and etc. Of these, the scenic spot preserved most completely is the Qu Yuan Temple. Green trees, fragrant flowers, quaint buildings and the solemn statue bring up the special features of Qu Yuan Structures.

Heimat von Qu-Yuan

　　Der Geburtsort von Qu-Yuan befindet sich in der Lepingli des Sanlü-Dorfes in Qu-Yuan-Gemeinde in Kreis Zigui. Und die Qu-Yuan-Gemeinde liegt an nördlichen Ufer des Tals von Militärbuch und Schwert in westlicher Strecke der Westgrabschlucht. Von Qu-Yuan-Gemeinde ab kann man mit einer Fahrt von 1 Stunde in Lepingli ankommen. Nach der Wasserspeicherung in Sanxia-Anlage bis Höhe von 139m kann man per Schiff von Jia-Jia-Dian bei Xiangxi-Fluß in die Sieben-Li-Schlucht und weiter durch das Sieben-Li-Tal fahren, dann kommt ein ausgedehntes Gelände entgegen, das Lepingli ist.

　　Kommt man in Lepingli ein, kann er sehen, daß ein majestätisches Schild mit Schriften Lepingli von den Orangenbäumen umringt wude. Es würde sagen, daß Sie in den Geburtsort des Großers einer Zeit angekommen sind! Hier sind viele Sehenswürdigkeiten im Zusammenhang mit Qu-Yuan. Im Altertum hatte man "acht Sehenswürdigkeiten gezählt", nämlich den Qu-Yuan-Tempel, Spiegeln-Brunen, Platz mit Weihrauchgefäß und Lesen-Höhle usw. Davon ist Qu –Yuan-Tampel am bestem erhalten. Die dunkelgrünen Bäumen, duftenden Blumen, altertümische Gebäude, majestätische Statue bilden alle den Stil mit charakterischen Merkmalen von Qu –Yuan Archtektur.

63

64

63　屈原廟　　　　64　樂平裏的屈原廟　　　　65　樂平裏牌坊
63　Qu Yuan's Hometown　64　Qu Yuan Temple in Lepingli　65　The Gateway of Lepingli
63　Heimat von Qu-Yuan　64　Qu-Yuan-Tempel in Lepingli　65　Gedenkbogen in Lepinli

66

66 昭君村
66 Zhaojun Village
66 Zhaojun-Dorf

▨ 昭君故里

"群山萬壑赴荆門，生長明尚有村。" 杜甫詩中所説的明妃村位于湖北省興山縣香溪河畔的寶坪村，歷代相傳是我國民族和睦使者和古代四大美女之一王昭君的故鄉。

王昭君，名嬙，興山縣人，漢元帝時因才貌出衆，入宮爲妃，封爲昭君。晋代避明帝司馬昭之諱，改稱明妃，傳説在入選時，她因未賄賂畫師，故像被丑化而不得寵，致深居冷宮數載。競寧元年（公元前33年），匈奴呼韓邪單于請求和親，願與漢永結友好，昭君自請嫁給他，臨行時，元帝才發現其容貌光彩照人，意欲留之，但難以失信，爲結束邊疆戰争，决定許嫁，元帝爲了表彰昭君，則改年號爲競寧。

三峽工程蓄水139米水位后，對昭君故裏的探訪不僅没有影響，反而便利了一些，游客乘船從西陵峽的西口處的香溪河口進入，直抵興山縣峽口鎮碼頭，再驅車近10公裏便可到達。

▨ Wang Zhaojun's Hometown

The poet Du Fu once wrote these lines, "Having scaled mountain after mountain on the way to Jingmen, you find the village where the village where the Illustrious Imperial Concubine was born." The village referred to above is located at Baoping Village beside the Xiangxi River in Xingshan County, Hubei Province. According to legend, the village is the hometown of Wang Zhaojun°™°™an envoy for national peace and also one of the four top beauties in ancient China.

Wang Zhaojun, also named Qiang, was from Xingshan County. In the Han Dynasty, she was chosen to be the imperial concubine for her wisdom and beauty, conferred a title of Zhoujun. In the Jin Dynasty, her name was changed to Mingfei to avoid to break a taboo with King Ming's name Sima Zhao. According to legend, when she was put on the list of candidate concubines, she was made a poor picture of her by the painter, because she didn't bribe him. So she failed to get into the emperor's good favour for several years. In 33 B.C., Huhanye, leader of the Xiongnu tribe, asked for marriage with an imperial woman and would like to make good friendship with Han forever. Zhaojun volunteered to marry him. Before her departure, King Yuan found how beautiful she was and wanted to let her stay on. But he couldn't lose trust. King Yuan decided to permit the marriage to end the wars in the border areas. In order to memorize Zhaojun, King Yuan changed his reign to "Jingning".

After the reservoir water lever rose to 139 meters, to visit Wang Zhaojun's hometown isn't affected. Instead, it is more convenient than before. You can take a ship from the mouth of the Xiangxi River at the west mouth of the Xiling Gorge, directly to the dork of Xiakou Town in Xingshan County. Then it will take only a 10 kilometers' drive to get there.

Geburtsort von Zhao-Jun

"Tausend Berge und Täler gehen nach Jingmen, wo ist die Ming-Fei (kaiserliche Konkubine) im Dorf angewachsen". Das in diesem Gedicht von Du-Fu aus Tang-Dynastie erwähnten Ming-Fei –Dorf heißt heute Baoping-Dorf. Es befindet sich am Xiangxi-Fluß in Kreis Xingshan der Provinz Hubei. Nach dem von mehren Generationen überlieferten Sagen ist hier die Heimat von Wang Zhaojun, die Gesandte für Frieden unserer Nation und auch eine der Vier Schönheitsfrauen im Altertum Chinas war..

Wang Zhaojun, namens Qiang, aus dem Kreis Xingshan. Sie war sehr schön und talentiert. In der Zeit des Yuan- Kaisers der Tang-Dynastie wurde Qiang zur Konkubine des Kaisers angenommen und ins Palast gebracht sowie mit dem Titel "Zhaojun" belehnt. Später wurde Zhaojun wegen des Tabus von dem Ming-Kaiser Si Ma-Zhao der Jin-Dynastie als Ming-Fei genannt. Dem Sagen nach würde Zhaojun von dem Maler, der für sie ein Porträt malen sollte, verheßlicht, weil sie den Maler nicht bestechen wollte, so Zhaojun den Kaisers Gunst nicht genießen konnte und mehr Jahre in kaltem Palast (ein Palast, in dem in Ungnade gefallene Kaiserinnen oder kaiserliche Konkubinen leben) leben mußte. Im ersten Jahre von Jinning (33 Jahre v.Z) wollte der Hunnenhauptling Huhanxie mit Han-Dynastie dauernd friedlich koexistieren und bat die Han-Dynastie um politische Heirat. Zhaojun bot sich zur Heirat mit diesem Hauptling. Kurz vor der Abreise nach Hunnen bemerkte Yuan-Kaiser, daß Zhaojun eigentlich so schön war. Er wollte sie haben, aber konnte sein Versprechen nicht brechen. Um den Krieg an der Grenze zu beenden, hatte sich der Kaiser entschloßen, diese Heirat zu genehmiegen. Um Zhaojuns Tat auszuzeichnen, hatte der Kaiser den Nahme des Jahres als Jinning (Streben nach Frieden) geändert.

Nach der Wasserspeicherung in Sanxia-Anlage bis die Höhe von 139m wird nicht nur keinen negativen Einfluß an der den Besuch von Zhaojuns Heimat ausüben, sondern im Gegenteil wird der Verkehr noch mehr günstig. Der Besucher kann bei Xiangxi-Flußmündung an westlicher Mündung von Westgrabschlucht an Bord gehen und per Schiff direkt zu dem Kai von Xiakou-Gemeinde im Kreis Xingshan fahren. Dann muß umsteigen und per Fahrzeug ca.10 km weiter fahren.

67 王昭君塑像
67 The Statue of Wang Zhaojun
67 Statue von Wang Zhaojun

68 王昭故裏
68 Wang Zhaojun's Hometown
68 Geburtsort von Zhao-Jun

西陵峽

西陵峽位于長江三峽的東端，它西至湖北的秭歸縣香溪河口，東至湖北宜昌市的南津關，全長66公裏，這是三峽中最長的一個峽。西陵峽又分爲東西兩個峽段，中間爲長約31公裏的廟南寬穀所分割，聞名中外的長江三峽工程就在這裏橫空出世；西段包括兵書寶劍峽、牛肝馬肺峽和崆嶺峽；東段包括燈影峽和黃貓峽。

西陵峽曾以灘多水急而著稱。著名的新灘和崆嶺灘均在西陵峽內，看大江急流，泡漩翻滾，激浪衝天，驚駭萬狀，歷史上，許多船只在這晨葬身洪濤；解放后，經過多年的整治，航道已得到了治理，尤其是葛洲壩水電工程的完工，這已經成爲歷史，從而結束了"三峽千古不夜航"的歷史，今日的西陵峽東西段分屬于葛洲壩水利樞紐和三峽工程的平湖庫區，輪船行駛在峽裏風平浪靜，碧波蕩漾，一切顯得舒坦而又清逸。

三峽工程蓄水139米水位之后，著名景點兵書寶劍峽和牛肝馬肺峽的一些象形物鐘乳石已全部沉入江中，明清古鎮孝莊村也被拆成一片瓦礫而永沉江底，似乎要抹掉三峽人心中美好的記憶。長江衝出西陵峽東口的南津關，便是湖北省的宜昌市，過宜昌市就進入了江漢平原和楚文化的發祥地。

Xiling Gorge

Located at the east end of the Yangtze Three Gorges, the Xiling Gorge starts from the mouth of the Xiangxi River in Zigui, Hubei Province in the west, ends at Nanjin Pass in Yichang in the east. With the total length of 66 kilometers it ranks the longest gorge in the Three Gorges. It consists of two sections, the east and the west, separated by the 31-kilometer-long Miaonan Broad Valley in the middle, where the famous Yangtze Three Gorges Project was born into the world. The west section includes the Tactics Book and Sword Gorge, the Ox Liver and Horse Lung Gorge and the Kongling Gorge. The east section includes the Shadow Play Gorge and the Yellow Cat Gorge.

The Xiling Gorge was noted for numerous shoals and speedy currents. Two famous shoals, Xintan Shoal and Kongling Shoal, are all in the Xiling Gorge. Look back to the past, the Yangtze River rushed rapidly and the rolling foams and raging waves were soul-stirring. In history, many ships and boats sank into the roaring waves. After liberation, the channel has been harnessed after being dredged for many years. Especially after the construction of the Gouzhouba Hydropower Project, all these have been in history. The history that, "the Three Gorges could not be navigated at night since remote past" ended. Now the east and west two sections of the Xiling Gorge separately belong to the Gezhouba Key Water Conservancy Project and the reservoir of the Three Gorges Project. Now here, the winds have subsided and the waves have calmed down. Ships and boats sail on green ripples. All these appear comfortable and carefree.

After the water level rose to 139 meters, some stalactites in the famous scenic spots Tactics Book and Sword Gorge and Ox Liver and Horse Lung Gorge, were completely submerged into the river. Xiaozhuang Village, the ancient town built in the Ming and Qing Dynasties, was taken apart and submerged too. The wonderful memories seemed to be wiped off the hearts of the people of the Three Gorges. Out of Nanjin Pass at the east mouth of the Xiling Gorge, there comes Yichang. Past Yichang, the Yangtze River enters the Jianghan Plain and the source of the Chu Culture.

WestgrabSchlucht

Westgrabschlucht liegt am östlichen Ende der Sanxia-Schluchtder Changjiang-Flußes. Sie streckt sich westlich bis Xiangxi-Flußmündung im Kreis Zigui der Provinz Hubei, und östlich bis Nanjing-Paß in Stadt Yichang der Provinz Hubei. Sie hat eine Gesamtlänge von 66km. Und diese ist die längste der Drei Schluchten des Changjiang-Flußes. Westgrabschlucht teit sich in westliche Strecke und östliche Strecke. In der Mitte wurde der Westgrabschlucht durch das breite Miaonan-Flußtal mit einer Länge von cs. 31km geschnitten. Die weltbekannte Sanxia-Anlage des Changjiang-Flußes ist hier zur Welt gekommen. Die westliche Strecke der Westgrabschlucht umfaßt die Schlucht von Militärbuch und Schwert, Schlucht von Rinderleber und Pferdlungen sowie Kongling-Schlucht, und die östliche Strecke schließt die Schlucht von Schatten unter Lampe, Schlucht von Gelbkatze.

Westgrabschlucht war duch viele Untiefe und reißendes Wasser bekannt. Die berühmte Neue Sandbank und Kongling-Sandbank befinden sich alle in Westgrabschlucht. Gegenüber dem reißenden Strom, dem umwalzenden Strudel, den turmhohen Wellen kann man von panischer Angst erfüllt werden. Man kann annehmen, wieviel Boote oder Schiffe in der Gechicht hier in den Wogen untergegangen waren. Nach der Befreiung wurde der Schiffahrtsweg durch mehrjährige Regulierung viel verbessert, besonders mit der Fertigstellung der Strom- und Wasser-Anlage bei Gezhoubao-Staudamm wurde die Geschichte "Seit tausend Jahren keine Nachtschiffährt in Sanxia-Schlucht" beendet. Heute gehören die West- und Oststrecken der Westgrabschlucht getrennt zu dem Flachstausee von Wasserbau-Schlüßelprojekt und Sanxia-Projekt. Das Schiff fährt hier durch die Schlucht in Ruhe und Frieden. Die kleinen Wellen kräuseln sich. Alls scheint so bequem und vornehm.

Nach der Wasserspeicherung in Sanxia-Anlage bis die Höhe von 139m sind manche Zeichentropfsteine von Schlucht von Militärbuch und Schwert sowie Schlucht von Rinderleber und Pferdlungenin den Fluß versunken. Das altertümische Dorf aus Ming-und Qing-Dynastie wurde auch abgerißen und ist mit in Schutt und Asche ewig im Fluß versunken sowie wird dort immer bleiben, ob es die schöne Erinnerung in unserem Kopf abwischen will. Aus dem Najing-Paß, wo der Changjiang-Fluß aus der östlichen Mündung stürzte, ist die Stadt Yichang der Provinz Hubei zu sehen. Nach Stadt Yichang kommt man in Jianghan-Ebene, wo die Wiege der antiken Kultur vom Chu-Reich ist.

69 西陵春色
69 Xiling Gorge in Spring   69 Frühling in Westgrabschlucht

70　西陵峡航拍
70　A Photo of Xiling Gorge
Shot in the Air
70　Westgrabschlucht aus
Luftphotographie

71 春意盎然
71 Fascinating Spring
71 Überall beherrscht Frühlingsstimmung

72 牛肝馬肺峡
72 Ox Liver and Horse Lung Gorge
72 Schlucht von Rinderleber und Pferdlungen

73　天生橋
73　The Innate Bridge
73　Brücke der Natur

74　西陵唱晚
74　Xiling Gorge in Sunset Glow
74　Nachtsgesang in Westgrab Sohlucht

75　西陵春色
75　Xiling Gorge in Spring
75　Frühling in Westgrabschlucht

■ 九畹溪漂流

　　九畹溪位于長江西陵峽西段牛肝馬肺峽的南岸, 距稱歸新縣城與三峽大壩僅20公裏, 這條長42.3公裏的自然秀美的小溪, 如今是新三峽旅游令游客最爲刺激的漂流探險旅游景區, 九畹溪溪水清澈, 兩岸山勢巍峨, 給人一種清新高雅之美。

　　游客在九畹溪13.2公裏的漂游途中會遇着許多驚心動魄之處, 落差90米, 河灘20多處, 讓你心跳, 讓你豪邁, 但有驚無險, 這正是她的魄力所在。同時, 你也會任皮艇悠哉游哉, 在碧澈的溪水裏最平靜的流淌, 五彩光滑的卵石在水波中熠熠閃爍, 尾尾游魚追逐着激灩的波光。橡皮艇從鳥語花叢和猿猴啼鳴的樹林中穿越, 你會體驗一種激情難抑的野趣。

■ Rafting on the Jiuwan Stream

　　The Jiuwan Stream locates on the south bank of the Ox Liver and Horse Lung Gorge in the west section of the Xiling Gorge in the Yangtze River, only 20 kilometers far from the new Zigui and the Three Gorges Project. The graceful stream, which is 42.3 kilometers long, is now the most exciting scenic spot for visitors to raft and explore in the tour of the new Three Gorges. The Juiwan Stream, with clear waters and lofty mountain on both banks, shows us a delicate and graceful beauty.

　　On the rafting journey of 13.2 kilometers along the Jiuwan Stream, you can experience many soul-stirring feelings. The falling head is more than 90 meters, and there are also more than 20 shoals in the stream, which let you tremble with fear, let you pride. But in fact, there is no danger after startling. This is just the charm of the stream. Sometimes you are even able to drift by a rubber boat on green and clear stream smoothly. The colorful smooth egg-stones are shinning in the waves. Batches of fishes are chasing the brilliant light of the waves. Passing through the flowers and woods, hearing birds singing and monkeys crowing, you will experience an exciting mild interest.

■ Schwimmen mit Strom über Jiuwan-Bach

　　Jiuwan-Bach befindet sich an der Südufer Schlucht von Rinderleber und Pferdlungen in westlicher Strecke der Westgrabschlucht des Changjiang-Flußes und entfernt sich von Neue Stadt Zigui sowie von Sanxia-Staudamm nur 20 km. Dieser Bach ist 42.3km lang und mit schöner Natur wurde er zu einem touristischen Gebiet für anreizendes Schwimmen mit Strom und Expedition gemacht. Das klare Bachwasser und die steil emporragende Berge bieten uns eine frische und vornehme Schönheit an.

　　Beim Schwimmen mit Strom über dem Jiuwan Bach wird man unterwegs viele erschütternden Szenen entgenkommen, z.B.der Wsserfall mit Falltief von 90m, 20 Untiefe, die würden Sie tief beunruhigen, aber dabei können Sie sich heroisch fühlen. Deren Anziehungskraft besteht grade darin, daß sie schreklich aber nicht gefährlich sind. Zugleich können Sie auch frei dem Schlauchboot anheimstellen und an dem klarem Wasser ruhig schwingen,. sogar die funkelnden glatten Buntkiesel und nach glitzerndem Wellenkräusel bewundern. Als das Schlauchboot unter einem Chorgesang von Vögeln und Affen mit Blumenduft durch grünen Wald schwimmt, werden Sie eine unüberwindbare Freude für Wildnis fühlen.

76 激流探險
76 Torrent Exploration
76 Expedition mit dem reissenden Strom

鳳凰山

秭歸新縣城鳳凰山景區是新三峽旅游的重要景點，也是"高峽出平湖"后新三峽旅游的起始點，三峽庫區蓄水后，鳳凰山變成了一個美麗的半島。鳳凰山地理位置獨特，與三峽大壩相距一公裏，在這裏觀賞三峽大壩的雄姿和高峽平湖勝景，總能讓游客激情燃燒。

爲了紀念屈原，展示峽江文明，鳳凰山正在建設的屈原公園，其主體建築有屈原祠、天問臺、博物館和楚風樓等，鳳凰山還是古建築的復建區，這裏正在復建24處峽江民居和文物，形成人與自然和歷史與現實交相輝映的意境，當游客穿行在那些已經落成或仍在復建中的峽江民居之中，遙看三峽大壩，仿佛已進入了歷史的時空遂道。

每逢端午節，在鳳凰山下的一帶水域，秭歸人仍以龍舟競渡這種獨特的方式，來紀念世界文化名人屈原。

Phoenix Mountain

The Phoenix Mountain in the Zigui Town is an important scenic spot, and the start of the tour of the new Three Gorges after "a smooth lake rises in high gorges". After the Three Gorges Project stored water, the Phoenix Mountain has been a beautiful peninsula. It takes a unique geologic position, only one kilometer far from the Three Gorges Dam. Here, enjoying the magnificent charisma of the Three Gorges Project and the beautiful view of the smooth lake rising in high gorges, always let one feel a thrill through his body.

To memorize Qu Yuan and show the civilization of the Gorges and River, the Qu Yuan Park is being built on the Phoenix Mountain. Its main buildings are the Qu Yuan Temple, the Sky-asking Platform, the museum and the Chu Folkway Tower, and etc. The Phoenix Mountain is also the region where the 24 ancient residential buildings and cultural relics are being repaired and rebuilt, where forms a harmonious atmosphere between human being and nature, history and reality. Walking through the residential buildings in the Gorge and River completed or being rebuilt, enjoying the distant view of the Three Gorges Dam, just seems to enter a thoroughfare of time and space of history.

On the Double fifth Festival (the fifth day of the fifth lunar month) every year, on the water area beside the foot of the Phoenix Mountain, the Zigui people still commemorate Qu Yuan in a unique method of staging dragon-boat races.

Phönixberg

Das Landschaftgebiet von Phönixberg in Neu Kreistadt Zigui ist eine wichtige touristische Senenswürdigkeit von Neuen Drei Schluchten und auch der touristische Ausgangspunkt, nachdem "Hochschluchten in Flachsee" wandelt wurde. Nach der Wasserspeicherung in Sanxia-Stausee ist der Berg eine schöne Halbinsel geworden. Der Phönixberg hat eine einzige geographische Lage und entfernt sich von Sanxa-Staudamm 1km. Man wird immer leidenschaftlich, wenn er hier die Majestät von Sanxia-Staudamm und die Schönheit bewundert.

Zum Gedenken an Qu-Yuan und zur Präsentation der Zivilisation von Schluchten des Changjiang-Flußes wird das Qu-Yuan-Park an dem Phönixberg gebaut.

Davon sind die Hauptteile: Qu-Yuan-Tempel, Himmelfragebüne, Museum und Gebäude für Kultur von Chu-Reich. Der Phönixberg ist auch ein Gebiet für Wiederanbau der altertümischen Archtektur. Hier werden 24 Whonungsgebäude und Kulturdenkmale wiederangebaut, um einen künstlerischen Gedanken von Integration der Menschen mit Natur sowie Geschichte mit Realität zu schaffen. Wenn man duch solche fertiggestellten oder noch zu bauenden Wohngebäude wandert und witer von ferne den Sanxia-Staudamm schaut, wäre er in einen historischen Zeit-Raum-Tunnel eingetreten.

Zu Gedenken an berühmten Weltliteraten Qu-Yuan wird bei dem jährlichen Drachenbootsfest an dem Gewässer an Phönixberg in Zigui immer eine Drachenbootswettfahrt versantaltet.

77 鳳凰山觀高峽平湖
77 Appreciating the Smooth Lake in the High Gorges on Phoenix Mountain
77 Auf Phönixberg die Hochschlucht und Flachsee anschauen

78 鳳凰山古建築
78 Ancient Architecture on Phoenix Mountain
78 Archtektur in Altertum von Phönixberg

79 龍舟競渡
79 Dragon – Boat Race
79 Drachenbootswettfahrt

78

79

■ 泗溪

泗溪距秭歸新縣城和三峽大壩西南 12 公裏，泗溪生態旅游區也是新三峽一個重要的旅游景區，它是由大溪、小溪、巴蕉溪和順陽溪等四條小溪組成，因而取名爲"泗溪"，總面積 20 平方公裏。

泗溪山穀幽深静謐，小橋流水、山巒叠嶂，植被茂密，物種繁多，尤其是山間石罅和小畔池旁到處是竹葉婆娑，連吹來的輕風中都象裹挾着竹的清香。景區内分布着 200 多個種類的竹子，形成了泗溪獨特的竹文化。

泗溪風景區最有特色的景觀是三吊水高山瀑布，這是我國近來發現的跌水落差最大的瀑布，總落差爲 389 米，共分五級飛流直下，跌落懸崖下無底的深潭之中，水花亂瓊碎玉般迸濺開來，化作縹緲的水霧，令人置身于一種虛幻的仙境之中。

■ Sixi (Four Streams)

Sixi Eco Reserve is 12 kilometers far from the southwest of the Zigui Town and the Three Gorges Dam. It is also an important scenic spot in the new Three Gorges. Covering an area of about 20 square kilometers, the Sixi Eco Reserve consists of four steams— the Great Stream, the Small Stream, the Banana Stream and the Shunyang Stream. So it is called as Sixi, which means "four streams".

In the deep valleys of Sixi Eco Reserve, there are small bridges above the flowing streams, continuous mountains, thick vegetation and various species. Here and there, among rocks, on mountains or beside ponds, you can see bamboo leaves swaying in the breeze. Even in the breeze, there seems to be faint scent of bamboos. The Eco Reserve is covered by about 200 kinds of bamboos. All these form the unique Bamboo Culture of Sixi.

The most characteristic scenic spot in the Eco Reserve is the Shandiaoshui Waterfall, which is discovered in our country as a waterfall with the highest falling head. The total falling head is 389 meters. It drops straightly by five steps into a bottomless deep pool, scattering in all ways like broken jades, changing into illusory fogs of water. Visitors seem to be placed in an unreal fairyland.

Sixi-Bach

Sixi-Bach entfernt sich von Neuer Kreisstadt Zigui und von Südwestteil des Sanxia-Staudamm 12km. Das ökologische touristische Landschaftsgebiet von Sixi ist auch eine wichtige Besichtigungspunkt von Neuer Sanxia-Schlucht.

Sixi-Bach besteht aus Großbach, Kleinbach, Bananenbach und Shunyang-Bach, und so bekommt er den Name "Sixi (Vier Bäche)". Die gesamte Bodenfläche von Sixi beträgt 20km².

Sixi verfügt über tiefe und ruhige Schluchten, kleine Brücke, unter der das Wasser fließt, wellenförmige Berge, dichte Pflanzendecke mit einem reichen Sortiment, besonders wachsen überall um die Steinblöcke und an Wasserteich die Bambusse, und die Bambusblättern verbreiten deren Duft in die Luft, so daß der sanften Wind auch nach Bambusduft riecht. In diesem Landschaftsgebiet wachsen Bambusse von mehr als 2000 Sorten, woduch ist die einzige charakterische Sixi-Kultur entstanden.

Die besonderste Sehenswürdigkeit in diesem Sixi-Landschaftgebiet ist der Sandiaoshui-Wasserfall, dessen gesamte Falltiefe von 389m ist am gößten in China, und der wurde in letzter Zeit entdeckt. Dieser Wasserfall fällt in fünf Stufen in den tiefen Teich unter dem überhängenden Felsen herunter, und die Gischt spritzt in alle Richtungen wie Jadeblöckchen und wandelt sich in Wassernebel. Und sie müßte uns in einem illusorischen Palast geführt haben.

80 泗溪風光
80 Sixi (Four Streams)
80 Sixi-Bach

81 三吊水瀑布
81 Sandiaoshui Waterfall
81 Sandiaoshui-Wasserfall

黄陵廟

距三峽大壩幾公裏處，位于廟南寬穀中黄牛峽南岸的黄牛山脚下，臨江聳立着一座紅墻黄瓦和金碧輝煌的古建築，這就是三峽中年代最久遠的古建築黄陵廟。

黄陵廟，原名黄牛祠、黄牛廟。相傳此廟是春秋時代爲了紀念神女助禹開峽的功績而修建。宋朝文學家歐陽修任夷陵（今宜昌）縣令時，只信禹王開山之功，認爲神牛助禹開峽的傳説純屬無稽之談，故將"黄牛廟"改名爲"黄陵廟"。

黄陵廟初建時，氣勢十分的宏偉。"廟前游客拜且舞，擊鼓吹笙屠白羊"。香火極旺，后因屢遭戰爭毀壞，幾經重建，雖不如初建，却仍然是三峽中規模最大的古建築，現僅存明萬曆四十六年（公元1618）重修的禹王殿、武候祠等。

禹王殿富麗堂皇，鬥拱飛檐，陶瓦獸脊，由36根大楠木立柱支撑，殿前高懸着兩塊木匾。其中有清慈禧太后所書的"砥定江瀾"和署名惠王所書"玄功萬古"。殿外立有《黄牛廟記》石碑、相傳爲諸葛亮所撰寫。

Huangling Temple

Several kilometers far from the Three Gorges Dam, located at the foot of the Yellow Cow Mountain at the south bank of the Yellow Cow Gorge in the Miaonan Broad Valley, there stands splendid ancient buildings with red walls and yellow titles, which was built in the earliest time in the Three Gorges— the Huangling Temple.

The Huangling Temple, originally called as the Huangniu Temple (the Temple of Yellow Cow). According to legend, it was built in the Spring and Autumn Period to memorize the yellow cow that had ever helped King Dayu to excavate the gorges. When the writer Ouyang Xiu in the Song Dynasty served as the county magistrate of Yiling (present Yichang), he renamed the temple as the Huangling Temple, because he thought all the achievements of excavating the gorges was only done by the King Dayu, but not the yellow cow. During the beginning period, the Huangling Temple was very magnificent, which attracted a great number of pilgrims. A poem says, "in front of the temple, visitors pilgrimize and dance, striking drums, playing 'sheng' (a kind of national music instrument of China) and killing sheep". Then it was destroyed in several wars. After being rebuilt several times, it was not as magnificent as before, but it is the largest scale group of ancient buildings in the Three Gorges, of which, only the Hall of King Dayu and the Wuhou Shrine rebuilt in 1618, were preserved.

The Hall of King Dayu is very splendid with zigzag arches and sticking-up eaves, supported by 36 pillars. On the top of the hall, two big plagues are hanging there. One says, "The mountains ease the billows" written by Queen Mother Cixi. The other says, "Contributing shines forever", on which there is a signature "written by King Hui". Out of the hall, there stands a stone tablet "Notes of the Huangniu Temple", which was said written by Zhuge Ling.

18Shipai & "The Family of the Three Gorges"

Gelbgrab-Tempel

An einem Ort, der sich von Sanxia-Staudamm einige Kilometer entfernt, und gegenüber dem Fluß am Gelbrind- Bergfuß an der Südufer der Gelbrind-Schlucht im Miaonan-Flußtal ragt ein in leuchtenden Farben erstrahlendes altertümisches Gebäude mit roten Wänden und gelben Dachziegeln. Dies ist der Gelbgrab-Tempel, die älteste altertümische Archtektur von Sanxia-Schlucht.

Gelbgrab-Tempel, früher als Geldrind-Kloster, Gelbrind-Tempel genannt. Der Legende nach wäre dieser Tempel zum Gedenken einer Gelbrinde, die dem Yu bei der Schöpfung der Schluchten geholfen hätte, in Zeit der Frühlings- und Herbstperiode gebaut. Aber in Song-Dynastie erkannte Ou-Yang-Xiu, der Schriftsteller als der Kreisvorsteher von Yiling (heute Yichang) nur das Verdienst um Wasserbau und hielt die Hilfe von Geisterrind für Unsinn. Deswegen wurde der Name "Gelbrinde-Tempel" durch "Gelbgrab-Tempel" ersetzt.

Am Anfang war der Tempel voll von imposanter Majestät. Es war sehr lebhaft. "Vor dem Tempel beten und singen die Besucher, neben dem trommeln, flöten und Weißlamm schlachten die Geschäftemacher". Später wurde der Tempel im Krieg mehrmals zerstört, und auch mehrmals wiederangebaut. Er ist zwar nicht so gut wie der originale, aber ist die größte altertümische Archtektur. Heute sind nur Yu-König-Palast und Wuhou-Tempel im Orginale erhalten, die im Jahre vierzigsechs nach Ming-Kalender (1618 v.Z.) wiederangebaut wurden.

Der prächtige Yu-König-Palast mit Gruppen hölzerner Ochsenkopfkapitellen und Dachschwingung sowie Porzellandachziegeln und Verzierung von Porzellantieren wurde von 36 große Holzsäulen aus Nanmu-Hplz gestützt. An Eingang von Palast hängen hoch zwei mit Inschriften versehenen Holztafel. Davon ist eine mit Inschriften "Erfolgreich Unterdrückung der Flußwogen" von Kaisers Mutter Cixi und die andere von Hui-König "Unvorstellbarers Verdienst für alle Zeit". Draußen steht ein Gedenkstein mit Inschriften "Geschischte des Gelbrind-Tempel", und dem Sagen nach wurde dieser Text von Zhuge Liang geschrieben.

82 黄陵廟遠眺
82 A Distant View of Huangling Temple
82 Von weiter über den Gelbgrabtempel blicken

83 大禹塑像
83 The Statue of Da Yu
83 Statue von Dayu

84 黄陵廟院内一角
84 A Corner of Huangling Temple
84 Eine Ecke von Innen des Gelbgrabtempel

85 黄 陵廟大門
85 The Gate of Huangling Temple
85 Tor von Gelbgrabtempel

石牌·三峡人家

　　輪船過三峽大壩五級船閘后順流而下，過了南沱，駛出一片開闊的廟南寬穀，便進入了西陵峽東段的燈影峽。燈影峽出口處，長江急轉90度大彎，彎的南岸有一天然巨石，形如古代的令牌，故人們取名爲石牌。

　　石牌的山頂上有四塊崢嶸嵯峨的奇石，形似《西游記》裏的唐僧師徒四人，每當夕陽西下，這四塊奇峰怪石映于藍色的天幕上，船動景移，好似正在演出一場精彩的燈影戲，別有風趣，故人們特地給這段峽取名燈影峽。

　　由于石牌風景區位于三峽大壩與葛洲壩之間，因此它是新三峽旅游的中最爲著名的景區，亦是"二壩一峽"旅游綫的重要組成部分，它由龍進溪、燈影石、石牌古鎮、楊家溪漂游等七大景區構成，其中龍進溪裏的"三峽人家"景點最具特色。

Shipai & the Family of the Three Gorges

　　Passing through 5-stage ship locks of the Three Gorges Project, sailing downstream, past Natuo, out of the Miaonan Broad valley, the ship enters the Shadow Play Gorge in the east section of the Xiling Gorge. At the outlet of the Shadow Play Gorge, the Yangtze River takes a 90-degree turning urgently. On the south bank of the corner, there is a large natural rock, which looks like a plate token of authority in ancient times. So it is called as Shipai. On the top of the mountain of Shipai, there are four unique large rocks, which look like Monk Xuanzang and his three disciples, four characters in the Chinese mythological novel Journey to the West. Whenever the sun goes down, the four rocks reflect to the blue sky. Following the sail of the ship, the scenery moves too, which seems that a wonderful shadow play is going on. So this gorge was named "the Shadow Play Gorge".

　　For Shipai is located between the Three Gorges Dam and the Gezhouba Dam, it is the most famous scenic spot in the tour of the new Three Gorges, and also the important component of the tour of "Two Dams and A Gorge". It includes seven scenic spots such as the Longjin Stream, the Shadow Play Rocks, the ancient Shipai Town and the Yangjia Stream, and etc. Of these, "the Family of the Three Gorges" is the most characteristic.

Gedenksteine & Haushalte von Sanxia-Schlucht

　　Der Dampfer fährt durch fünfstufige Schleuse von Sanxia-Steusedamm und Natuo, dann weiter von dem Miaonan-Breittal aus in die Schlucht von Schatten unter Lampe, die östliche Strecke von Westgrabschlucht ist. An der Mündung der Schlucht von Schatten unter Lampe macht Changjiang-Fluß eine Wendung um 90 Grad. An südlicher Ufer dieser Wendung steht ein riesigr Stein in Form einer altertümischer Befehlstäfelchen, so nennt man dieser Stein als Gedenkstein.

　　Die an dem Stein hochragenden vier seltsamen Steine sind Äußern nach wie vier Helden im klassischen Meisterwerk Chinas "Die Pilgerfahrt nach dem Westen", nämlich der Mönch Tang mit seinen Lehrlingen. Wenn die Sonne untergeht, spiegeln sich diese vier Steine an dem blauen Himmel. Und mit der Bewegung von Schiff ändert sich auch die Szene. Es gleicht einer Vorführung von Schattenspiel. Deshalb hat man dieser Schluchtestrecke den Name Schatten unter Lampe gegeben.

　　Da sich das Gedenkstein- Landschaftsgebiet zwischen dem Sanxia-Stausedamm und dem Gezhouba-Stausedamm liegt, ist dieses die berühmteste Sehenswürdigkeit für Tourismus von Neuer Sanxia-Schlucht und auch der wichtigster Bestandteil der Reiselinie "Zwei Stausedämme mit einer Schlucht". Diese Linie

86

87

umfaßet sieben Landschaftszone, bzw. Longjin-Bach, Stein von Schatten unter Lampe, Gedeksteine von alter Gemeinde, Schwimmen mit Strom in Yangjia-Bach usw. Und davon ist die "Haushalte von Sanxia-Schlucht" von Longjin-Bach am besten charaterisiert.

86	石牌風景區	87	二峽第一彎	88	燈影石
86	Shipai Scenic Spot	87	The First Bend in the Three Gorges	88	Shadow Play Rocks
86	Landschaftszone von Gedenksteinen	87	ErsteBucht von Drei Schluchten	88	Stein von Schatten der Lampe

石牌·三峡人家

　　"三峡人家"景點依山傍水，風情如畫，傳統的三峽吊脚樓點綴于山水之間，久違的古帆船和烏篷船靜靜的地停泊在"三峽人家"的門前，千百年來流經不衰的民俗風情，體現着峽江人民的質樸好客，走進峽江吊脚樓，清秀美麗的三峽少女爲您捧上一杯峽州清茶，獻上一段土家族民俗歌舞，游客定會覺得如夢似幻，親切怡然。

Shipai & the Family of the Three Gorges

　　The scenic spot "the Family of the Three Gorges" is relying on the mountain and beside the stream. The scenery is just like a beautiful picture. The traditional hanging bases in the Three Gorges embellish the mountains and water. The ancient junk and black-covering boat stop silently in front of the Family of the Three Gorges. The folk customs handed down for thousands of years embody the simple and hospitable dispositions of the people of the Gorges and River. When you step into the hanging bases in the Gorges and River, slim girls will hold a cup of tea to you, and show a part of dance and song of the Tujia Minority. You will feel warm and comfortable as if you are dreaming.

Gedenksteine & Haushalte von Sanxia-Schlucht

　　Die "Haushalte von Sanxia-Schlucht" liegt am Fuß des Bergs und dicht bei dem Fluß. Die Landschaft hier ist so schön wie Malerei. Die traditionellen über einem Abhang vorspringenden Gebäude verteilen sich über die Landschaft mit Bergen und Flüßen. Das lange nicht zu sehene atertümische Segelschiff und Wupeng-Boot parken ruhig vor der Haustür von "Haushalte von Sanxia-Schlucht". Und die seit tausend Jahre nicht verfallenen Sitten und Gebräuche des Volkes verköpern die Naturlichkeit und Gastfreundlichkeit. Wenn Sie in das über dem Abhang vorspringenden Gebäude eintritt, reicht Ihnen ein Sanxia-Mändchen eine Tasse Schlucht-Tee und zeigt Ihnen ein Stück Tanz und Gesang. Sie würden sich wie im Traumwelt fühlen, so freunlich und angenehm.

89 黄龍瀑
89 Huanglong Waterfall
89 Gelbdrachenwasserfall

90 龍進溪瀑
90 Longjin Stream
90 Wasserfall vom Drachen ins Bach

91 三峡人家
91 Family of the Three Gorges
91 Haushalte von Sanxia-Schlucht

92 琴鷹瀑
92 Qinying Waterfall
92 Wasserfall von Geige und Adler

93 綠韵
93 Green Landscape
93 Andauender Reiz der Grüne

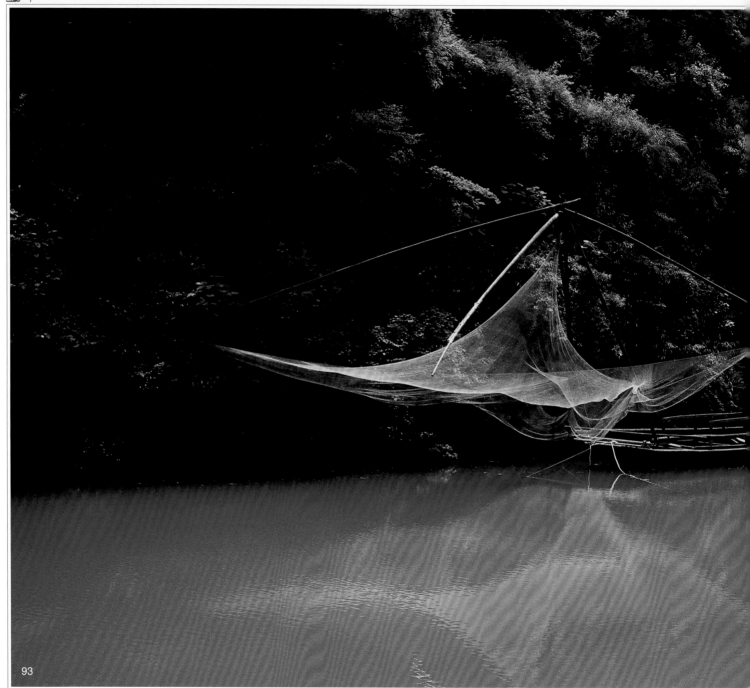

93

■ 三游洞

三游洞位于宜昌市峡口风景区西陵峡东口北岸的西陵山上，前有下牢溪，后有长江，是个高约6米，深宽各约二三十米的溶洞。唐代以前它还是一个无名的石灰岩溶洞，相传唐代元和十四年（公元819年），白居易与其弟白行简在宜昌和诗人元稹不期而遇，三人便相约同游此洞，并且每人赋诗一首，由白居易作《三游洞序》书于石壁，序云："以吾三人始游，故目为三游洞"。一百多年后，苏洵、苏轼和苏辙父子三人出川赴京城开封赶考，途经宜昌，也同游此洞，每人又赋诗一首。三游洞的名字就由此而来，后世在谈到三游洞的历史沿革时，以白氏兄弟和元稹之游为前三游，苏氏父子之游为后三游。现在洞内还有明代所刻白居易《三游洞序》碑等多种石刻。

三游洞本身并不以景致见长，但地理位置得天独厚，洞前高峡夹峙，有清澈可览的下牢溪绕而过与长江相接。使整个三游洞景区形成一个半岛，与长江三峡的西口白帝城半岛有惊人的相似之处，大自然的鬼斧神工造就出长江三峡这样的完美与统一。游人登上西陵山，可尽情地观赏南津关长江上、中游两种不同河段险夷交替的景色，同时，也可尽揽葛洲坝平湖的壮丽景观。

■ Three Visitors Cave

The Three Visitors Cave is situated on the Xiling Mountain in Xiakou scenic spot of Yichang on the north bank of the east mouth of the Xiling Gorge. In front of it is the Xialao Stream, and behind it is the Yangtze River. The Three Visitors Cave is a solution cavity, which is 6 meters high, about 20 or 30 meters deep and wide. It was only a limestone solution cavity without a name before the Tang Dynasty. As the legends has it, in 819 (in the 14th year of the Yuanhe reign of the Tang Dynasty), the great poet Bai Juyi and his younger brother Bai Xingjian met another poet Yuan Zhen by chance. They visited the cave together and each wrote a poem. Preface of Three Visitors Cave engraved on the cliff. The preface says, "we three persons visited the cave first, so we called it as Three Visitors Cave". About over 100 years later, Su Xun, Father Su Shi and Son Su Zhe came out of Sichuan to the capital Kaifeng to take part in the exam and passed Yichang. They visited this cave together and each wrote a poem too. So the cave was named as Three Visitors Cave. Speaking of the history, the visit of Brothers Bai and Yuan Zhen was called as "the former three visitors", the visit of Father and Son Sus was called as "the later three visitors". Now in the cave, there are various stone-carved inscriptions, such as the tablet Preface of Three Visitors Cave engraved in the Ming Dynasty.

The Three Visitors Cave is not famous for its natural view, but it has a key geographic position abound in gifts of nature. In front of the cave, lofty cliffs stand face to face, the clear

94

95

Xialao Stream flows around the cave to join the Yangtze River. So the whole scenic spot forms a peninsula. It is amazingly similar to Badi Town (White King Town) peninsula. The magic axe of nature brought up so perfect and harmonious Three Gorges. Climbing up to the Xiling Mountain, you can alternatively appreciate the two different sceneries of the upper position and middle position of the Three Gorges, dangerous or calm. At the same time, you can enjoy the splendid scenery of the reservoir of the Gezhouba Dam.

Höhle von Drei Reisenden

Die Höhle von Drei Reisenden befindet sich an dem Westgrabberg an Ostufer der östlichen Mündung von Westgrabschlucht in Stadt Yichang. Sie ist eine durch Korrosion gebildete Höhle mit einer Höhe von 6, Breite und Tiefe getrennt von ca..20-30m, und vor ihr liegt Xialau-Bach, und hinter ihr fließt Changjiang-Fluß. Diese Höhle war vor der Tang-Dynastie eine kleine und unbekannte korrosierte Höhle ohne Name. Dem Sagen nach sei Bai Juyi mit seinem Bruder Bai Xingjian im Jahre 14 von Yuanhe der Tang-Dynastie (819 n.Z.) dem Dichter Yuan-Zhen in Yichang zufällig begegenet. Die drei hätten eine Versprechung getroffen, zusammen diese Höhle zu besuchen und je ein Gedicht daüber zu schreiben. Und das von Bai Juyi geschiebene "Vorwort zu H?hle von Drei Reisenden" sollte an der Wand geschrieben werden. In diesem Vorword wurde geschrieben: "Da wir

drei diese Höhle besuchen, soll sie also die Höhle von Drei Reisenden heißen". Mehr als hundert Jahre danach gingen ein Vater namens Su Xun, Söhne Su Shi und Su Zhe von Sichuan nach Hauptstadt Kaifeng zur kaiserlichen Prüfung.Unterwegs besuchten Sie diese Höhle und hatten auch je ein Gedicht über diese Höhle geschrieben. Diese wurde diese Höhle bekannt gemacht. Wenn man später über die Geschichte der Höhle spricht, nennt man Reise von Baus Büdern und Yuan-Zhen die Frühe Drei Reise, und von Sus Vater und Söhnen die Spätere Drei Reisenden. Heute bestehen noch die Inschriften aus dem Text von Bai-Juyi "Vorwort zu Höhle von Drei Reisenden" an Gedenksteine aus Ming-Dynastie.

Die Landschaft von dieser Höhle ist nicht deren Vorteil, aber ihre geographische Lage ist außergewöhnlich. Vor der Höhle stehen sich zwei Schluchtenufer einander gegenüber, und das Xialao-Bach mit klarem Wasser fließt die Höhle um zu dem Changjiang-Fluß und womit macht das ganze Landschaftsgebiet von Höhle zu einer Halbinsel. Es gleicht erstaunlich der Halbinsel von Baidi-Stadt an westlicher Mündung der Sanxia-Schlucht des Changjiang-Flußes. Die Vollkommenheit und Einheit der Natur von Drei Schluchten des Changjiang-Flußes sind wie von dem Gott mit Hand geschaffen. An dem Westgrabberg kann man die Landschaft wechselnd mit gefährlichen und sicheren Szenen von unterschiedlichen Flüßtrecken im Ober- und Unterlan des changjiang-Flußes an Nanjing-Paß so wie den stattlichen Flachsee mit Gezhouba-Stausedamm bewundern.

94 下牢溪
94 Xialao Stream
94 Xialau-Bach

95 西陵峡口南津關
95 Nanjin Pass at the Mounth of Xiling Gorge
95 Nanjing-Paß ann Mündung der Westgrabschluchten

96 鳥瞰三游洞
96 A Bird's-Eye View of Three Visitors Cave
96 Höhle von Drei Reisenden aus Vogelperspektiv

97 楚塞樓
97 Chusai Tower
97 Chusai-Pavillon

98 三游洞古代題刻
98 Ancient Engraving Inscriptions in Three Visitors Cave
98 Inschriften in Altertum von Höhle von Drei Reisenden

99 三游洞内景
99 The Scenery inside Three Visitors Cave
99 Innenszene von Höhle von Drei Reisenden

97

98

99

葛洲壩水利樞紐工程

葛洲壩，是長江上第一座水利樞紐工程，它是由我國自行研究、設計和建設而成的大型水電站。它位于長江三峽的出口宜昌市城區，距西陵峽口的南津關2．3公裏，距上游三峽大壩38公裏。

長江之水衝出南津關之后，江面豁然開朗，由300米驟然展寬至2200多米，江水被江中的葛洲壩和西壩兩個小島分爲三股江水，水利樞紐工程就因建在葛洲壩而得名。

葛洲壩水利樞紐工程全長2606．5米，高70米，工區占地面積約9平方公裏，主要由攔水壩、三座船閘、兩座水力發電廠房、一座泄水閘、兩座衝沙閘和擋水墻組成。壩內有27孔泄洪閘，每秒可排泄11萬立方米特大洪水，發電裝機21臺，總裝機容量271．5萬千瓦，年發電量157億千瓦時，其發電送往上海、河南、湖南、武漢等地；葛洲壩有三座單級船閘，其中兩座可通過萬噸級的輪船，通航建築物年單向通過能力超過5000萬噸。

葛洲壩水利樞紐工程自1970年12月30日動工興建，1981年5月一期工程下閘蓄水，于1988年12月20日全面竣工，工程建設總投資48億元人民幣。葛洲壩經受了1981年和1998年兩次百年不遇的特大洪水的考驗，大壩安然無恙。

Gezhouba Key Water Conservancy Project

The Gezhouba Dam is the first key water conservancy project across the Yangtze River. It is a large-scale hydropower station, which was researched, designed and built by our own country. Located in the urban area of Yichang city at the exit of the Yangtze Three Gorges, the Gezhouba Dam is 2.3 kilometers far from Nanjin Pass at the mouth of the Xiling Gorge, and 38 kilometers far from the Three Gorges Dam in the upper position. After rushing out of Nanjin Pass, the Yangtze River suddenly becomes open and wide. Its width expands from 300 to over 2200 meters. The river was separated into three currents by two islands, Gezhouba and Xiba. The hydropower project was named for being built here.

The Gezhouba Hydropower Project is 2605.5 meters long and 70 meters high. Covering about 9 square kilometers, the station includes the dam across the river, 3 ship locks, 2 hydropower generation houses, a water spill lock and 2 sand wash locks and a water block wall. The 27-bay flood discharge lock can discharge a water volume of 110 thousand cubic meters per second. All 21 sets of generators with a total installed capacity about 2.715 million kW can generate electricity 15.7 billion kWh annually. The electricity is transported to Shanghai, Henan, Hunan, Wuhan and other big cities. There are three single-stage locks, of which, two can allow the passage of 10000-ton jumbo ships. The total annual single-way transportation capacity of the ship locks is over 50 million tons.

The project started on December 30, 1970. The first phase started to reserve water in May 1981. It was completed on December 20, 1998. The total investment of the project cost RMB4.8 billion yuan. Standing the test of the two historical heaviest floods happened in 1981 and 1998, the dam stayed safe and sound.

Gezhouba-Staudamm -Wasserbauschlüßelprojekt

Gezhouba-Staudamm, das erste Wasserbau-Schlüßelprojekt an dem Changjiang-Fluß, ist ein großes Kraftwerk, das von China selbst geforscht, konstruiert und gebaut wurde. Er bindet sich im Stadtgebiet von Yichang, die Ausgang von Drei Schluchten des Changjiang-Flußes ist, und entfernt sich von Nanjing-Paß an der Mündung der Westgrabschlucht 2.3km, von Sanxia-Staudamm im Oberlan 38km.

Von Nanjing-Paß aus erweitert der Schangjiang-Fluß seine Breite von 300m an 2200m. Hier wurde das Changjiang-Flußwasser durch Gezhouba-Staudamm und Weststausedamm in drei Strömen geteilt. Da das Wasserbau-Schlüßelprojekt hier gebaut wurd, bekommt es diesen Name.

Das Wasserbau-Schlüßelprojekt hat eine gesamte Länge von 2606.5m und die Höhe von 70m, den Arbeitsbreich von ca. 9km^3 . Es umfaßt Staüdämme, drei Schiffsschleusen, zwei Fabrikgebäude für Wasserkraftwerk, eine Auslaßschleuse, zwei Sandabspülungsschleusen und Wassersperrungswand. Die im Damm bestehenen 27 Auslaßschleusen können das besondere große Hochwasser 110,000m^3/Sekunde ablassen. Die 21 Generatoren mit einer installierter Kapazität von 2,715,000kW können jährlich den elektrischen Strom von 15.7Mrd.kW erzeugen, der nach Shanghai, Provinz Henan, Hunan, und Stadt Wuhan geleitet. Im Gezhouba-Staudamm bestehen auch 3 einstufige Schiffsschleuse, davon sind zwei passierbar für den Dampfer von 10,000tdw. Die einspurige Schiffahrtskapazität der befahrbaren Bauten kann jährlich 50,000,000t erreichen.

Gezhouba-Staudamm- Wasserbauschlüßelprojekt hat mit seinem Bau am 30. Dez. 1970 begonnen und in Mai 1981 wurde die Schleuse von erster Phase des Projekts für Wasserspeicherung geschloßen. Das Projekt mit einer gesamten Investition von 4.8Mrd.RMB wurde am 20.Dez. 1988 allseitig fertiggestellt. Gezhouba-Staudamm wurde zweimal durch Hochwasser, wie es seit hundert Jahren nicht mehr dagewesen ist, getrennt vom 1981 und 1998, erprobt.

100 葛洲南水利樞紐工程航拍（3000米高空）
100 A Photo of Gezhouba Key Water Conservancy Project Shot in the Air(3,000 meters high above the ground)
100 Wasserbauschlüßelprojekt bei Gezhounan aus Luftphotographie

100

宜昌市

宜昌市位于湖北省的西部和長江三峽的東口，地處長江中上游的結合部，湘鄂渝三省市交匯地，是新三峽旅游的起始點。宜昌上控巴蜀和下引荆襄，以"三峽門户"、"川鄂咽候"而著稱，爲歷代兵家必争之地。三國時期的夷陵之戰就發生在宜昌城區的長江西陵峽口。

宜昌，古稱夷陵，至今已有2400多年的歷史，因"水至此而夷，山至此而陵"得名，是楚文化和巴人文化的發祥地，世界歷史文化名人屈原和中國古代民族和睦的使者、古代四大美人之一王昭君均出身在這裏，自東漢以來，宜昌就是歷代洲、府所在地。全市共轄五縣三市（縣級）五區，總人口414. 93萬人，國土面積2. 1萬平方公裏，城區面積4249平方公裏，建成區面積61. 5平方公裏，城區人口133. 8萬人，是湖北省的第二大百萬人口的大城市。

三峽捧出宜昌市，世界崛起水電城，萬裏長江第一壩。葛洲水利樞紐工程就在宜昌城區，舉世聞名的三峽工程距城區僅38公裏，是湖北省最大的水電站清江隔河岩和高壩洲電站距城區只有50公裏，加上300多座星落棋布的中小電站，全市水電總裝機容量可達2300萬千瓦，在方圓不到100公裏的範圍内，擁有如此豐富的水電資源和如此充分的開發程度，在世界獨一無二的。被譽爲"世界水電之都"。

Yichang City

Yichang is located in the west of Hubei Province and at the east mouth of the Three Gorges. It is also at the conjunctional place of the middle and upper positions of the Yangze River. It is the place where Hunan, Hubei and Chongqing meet. It is the start of the tour of the new Three Gorges. "Yichang can easily control Sichuan in the upper position and leads to Jinzhou and Xiangyang downstream." Known as "the gate of the Three Gorges" and "the throat between Sichuan and Hubei", Yichang was a hot military place contested by all strategists in past dynasties. During the Three Kingdoms Period, the Yiling Campaign took place in urban area of Yichang at the mouth of the Xiling Gorge.

Yichang, called as Yiling in ancient times, has a long history of over 2400 years. It is the source of the Chu Culture and the Ba Man Culture. There gave birth the cultural famous man in the world, Qu Yuan, and the envoy for national peace and one of the four top beauties in ancient China, Wang Zhoujun. Since the Eastern Han Dynasty, Yichang was the seat of local prefecture and state in the past dynasties. Now the whole city governs 5 counties, 3 cities (county-level), and five districts. With a total population of 4.1493 million, it covers an area of 21000 square kilometers, of which, the urban area is 4249 square kilometers, the completed area 61.5 square kilometers. The urban population is 1.338 million. It is the second laregest million-population city in Hubei Province.

101 夷陵廣場
101 Yiling Square
101 Yiling-Platz
101

Three Gorges boost Yichang, a city featuring hydropower rises in the world! The first Dam across the long Yangtze River, the Gezhouba Key Water Conservancy Project is in the urban area of Yichang. The well-known Three Gorges is only 38 kilometers far from the urban area. The Geheyan Hydropower Station and Gaobazhou Hydropower Station in the Qingjiang River, the largest hydropower stations in Hubei Province, are only 50 kilometers far from the urban area. Together with other 300 small and medium sized hydropower stations, the total installed capacity of electricity of the whole city can reach 23 million kW. It's pretty rare in the world for such rich hydropower resources and developed exploration system centered in less than 100 square kilometers. Yichang lives up to a title "the world hydropower city".

Stadt Yichang

Stadt Yichang befindet sich an der westlichen Mündung der Sanxia-Schlucht des Changjiang-Flußes und im Westen der Provinz Hubei sowie am Verbindungsort von Ober- und Unterlan des Changjiang-Flußes, wo drei Provinzen einander grenzen, und ist auch der Ausgangspunkt von Sanxia-Schlucht-Reise. Yichang kneipt oben Ba und Schu (Abküßzung von Provinz Hubei und Sichuan), unten leitet in Jing und Xiang (Jingmen und Xiangyang). Sie ist als "Tor der Drei Schluchten", und "Kehle von Sichuan" bekannt. Sie war ein strategisch wichtiger Ort in allen Dynastien. Der alte Yiling-Krieg in der Zeit der Drei Reichen entstand hier an der Mündung der Westgrabschlucht des Changjiang-Flußes im Stadtgebiet Yichang.

Yichang, in alter Zeit Yiling genannt, hat eine Geschichte von mehr als 2400 Jahren, und den Namen aus dem Vers "Wasser bis hier ungefährlich (Yi), Berg bis zu Hügel (Ling)" bekommen. Sie ist der Ursprungsort der Chu-Kutur und Ba-Kultur. Der historisch berühte Welt-Literiat Qu-Yuan und die eine der Vier Schönsten, die Gesandte für Frieden der Nation im Altertum Chinas, waren hier geboren. Seit der Östlichen Han-Dynastie war Yichang die Residenz der Bezierks- und Kreisregierung aller Dynastien. Unter deren Verwaltung stehen 5 Kreise, 3 Städte (Kreisebene), 5 Bezierke. Mit einer Bevölkerung von 4,149,300 Personen, Landfläche von 21, 000km^2, Stadtgebietfläche von 4249 km^2, bebauter Stadtgebietsfläche von 61.5 km^2, städtischen Einwohner von 1,33.8,000 ist sie die zwei größte Stadt der Provinz Hubei, die über 1 Mio. Einwohner hat.

Drei Schluchten tragen die Stadt Yichang hervor, aus der Welt ragt die Wasser-und Stromstadt empor. Der erste Staudamm an dem Changjiang-Flußes von zhen tausen Li, das Gezhouba-Staudamm-Wasserbauschlüßeprojekt befindet sich im Stadtgebiet von Yichang. Das weltbekannte Sanxia-Schlucht-Projekt entfernt sich von dem Stadtgebiet nur 38 km; das Qingjiang-Wasserkraftwerk, das größte Wasserkraftwerk in Provinz ist, und das Gaobazhou-Kraftwerk entfernen sich auch nur 50km; samt mehr als 300 Mittel-und Großkraftwerken kann die gesamte installierte Leistung von 2,3 Mio.kW erreichen. Yichang muß die einzige, die auf einem Bereich von knapp 100km über so reiches Wasser-und Stromressourcen verfügt. Sie ist auch würdig, als "Wasser-und Stromstadt der Welt" gepreist zu werden.

102　夷陵長江大橋
102　Yiling Yangtze River Bridge
102　Yiling-Changjiang-Brücke

103　玉泉寺
103　Yuquan Temple
103　Jadequellentempel

104　關陵廟
104　General Guan's Temple
104　Guang-Kaisergabtempel

■ 長江三峽工程

新三峽之旅的最高潮之處無愧爲三峽工程，作爲當今世界上最大的水利工程，僅在施工方面，三峽工程就創下了多項世界之最，它擁有世界上級數最多，總水頭最高的內河船閘和世界規模最大，難度最高的升船機，隨着26臺70萬千瓦的發電機組組陸續投産，總裝機容量將達到1820千瓦，它還將成爲世界上最大的水電站。

長江三峽工程壩址位于湖北省宜昌市三鬥坪鎮中堡島，距下游葛洲壩工程38公裏，三峽工程采用"一級開發，一次建成，分期蓄水，連續移民"的方案。工程總工期17年，分三個階段施工，第一階段1993~1997年，爲施工准備及一期工程；第二階段1998~2003年，爲二期工程；第三階段2004~2009年，爲三期工程。三峽工程動態總投資預計爲2039億元人民幣，水庫最終將淹沒耕地43. 13萬畝，最終將移民113. 18萬人。

三峽工程竣工后，水庫正常蓄水位175米，防洪庫容221. 5億立方米，總庫容達393億立方米，可充分發揮其在長江中下游防洪體系中的關鍵性骨干作用，使荊江河段防洪標准由現在的十年一遇提高到百年一遇，是當今防洪效益最將顯著改善長江宜昌至重慶660公裏的航道，萬噸級船隊可直達重慶港，將發揮防洪、發電、航運、養殖、旅游、保護生態、净化環境、開發性移民、南水北調、供水灌溉等十大綜合效益，是目前世界上任何巨型電站無法比擬的！

■ Yangtze Three Gorges Project

The high tide of the tour of the Yangtze Three Gorges is doubtlessly the Three Gorges Project. As the greatest hydropower project in the world, only in construction, the Three Gorges created many top records in the world. It has the ship locks with the most stages and the highest total head in inland rivers. It has the most complex and largest scale ship elevators. After 26 units generators (the capacity of each unit is 700,000 kW) are put into produce in secession, the total installed capacities will reach 18.2 million kW. It will be the greatest hydropower station in the world.

The Three Gorges Project locates at the Zhongbao Island in Sandouping in Yichang, Hubei Province, which is about 38 kilometers far from the Gezhouba Project in the lower position. The whole construction of the project is done according to the plan of "the first class development, complete construction, reserving by steps and continuous immigrants". The total time limits for the project cost 17 years including 3 phases. The first phase started from 1993 and ended in 1997. The second phase is from1998 to 2003. The third phase is from 2004 to 2009. The total investment of the Three Gorges Project is estimated to be 203.9 billion yuan. At last, the reservoir will submerge about 28,753 hectares arable lands and force 1.1318 million people to migrate.

When the project is completed finally, the normal water level of the reservoir will reach 175 meters. The holding capacity for flood control is 22.15 billion cubic meters. The total holding capacity is 39.3 billion cubic meters. It can take full advantages of its key functions in flood control of middle and lower positions of the Yangtze River. The capacity of flood control in Jingjiang Dike, has been raised from the present standard of once-in-10-year to once-in-100-year. With the biggest benefits in the flood control, the Three Gorges Project will obviously improve the shipping conditions of the Yangtze River in the 660 kilometers course from Yichang to Chongqing. 10,000 tonnage ship groups are able to sail all the way up to Chongqing Harbor directly. It has ten general benefits including flood control, hydropower generation, shipping improvement, breed aquatics, tourism, eco protection, environment protection, redistribution, irrigation supply, and etc. So far, no other jumbo hydropower station in the world is comparable to it.

■ Sanxia- Schluchten des Changjiang-Flußes-Projekt

Der höchste Punkt der Reise bei Neuer Sanxia-Schlucht ist Sanxia-Schluchten-Anlage. Als das größte Wasserbauprojekt der heutigen Welt hat das Sanxia-Schluchen-Projekt nur bei der Bauausführung schon mehr Weltrekorde angestellt. Dieses Projekt verfügt über die Schiffsschleuse für Binnenfluß, die mit der Zahl der Stufen und mit der Höhe des Wasserkopfes an der Spitz der Welt ist, und das Schiffshebewerk, das mit dessen Größe und mit der Höhe des Schwirigkeitsgrades an erster Stelle der Welt steht. Mit der Inbetriebnahme mit Unterbrechungen der 26 Generatorenaggregate von 27kW kann die installierte Leistung 1820kW erreichen.

Der Sitz von Sanxia-Schluchten-Projekt des Changjiang-Flußes liegt auf der Zhongbao-Insel in Gemeinde Sandouping zu Stadt Yichang der Provinz Hubei und entfernt sich von Gezhouba-Staudann 38 km. Bei Sanxia-Schlucht-Projekt wird der Plan "Erschließung erster Klasse, Fertigstellung beim ersten Bau, Wasserspeicherung in Etappen, kontinuirliche Umsiednung" durchgeführt. Der Bautermin für das gesamte Projekt dauert 17 Jahre. Die Bauausführung wird in drei Zeitetappen erfolgt. Die erste Etappe ist von 1993 bis 1997 für Vorbreitung und den Bau der Ersten Phase, die zweite von 1998 bis 2003 für den Bau der Zweiten Phase, und die dritte Etappe für den Bau der Dritten Phase. Die gesamte dynamische Investition für Sanxia-Schluchten-Projekt wird schätzungsweise 203.9 Mrd RMB betragen. Und der Stausee wird schließlich die Ackerland von 431,300 Mu überschwemmen. Endlich werden 1,131.180 Einwohner umgezogen.

Nach Fertigstellung von Sanxia-Schlucht-Projekt wird der Stausee mit dem Normalwasserstand bei 175m, Wasserspeicherungsmöglichkeit zum Hochwasserschutz von 22.15Mrd. m³, und der gesamte Kapazität von 39.3 Mrd. m³ seine entscheidende Rolle der Hauptstütze im Schutzsystem gegen Hochwasser im Mittel-und Unterlauf des Changjiang-Flußes spielen, wodurch der Hochwasserschutzstandard von heute gegen das Hochwasser, wie es seit zehn Jahre einmal dagewesen ist, auf den gegen das, wie es seit hundert Jahre einmal dagewesen ist, bei Flußabschnitt in Jingiang erhöht werden kann. Dieser Stausee wird die effizienteste Hochwasserschutzanlage sein und den Schiffahrtsweg mit einer Länge von 660km von Yichang-Chongqing betrählich verbessern. Über diesem Stausee kann der Dampfer von 100,000tdw direkt nach Chongqiing hinfahren. Der Effekt, den dieser Stausee in zehn Bereichen bzw. Hochwasserschutz, Stromerzeugung, Schiffahrt, Zucht, Tourismus, Schutz des Ökosystems, Umweltreinigung, Umsiedlung zur Erschließung, "Wasser von Süden nach, Norden leiten", Waaserversorgung und Bewässerung, machen wird, ist unvergleichbar für alls riesigen Kraftwerke in gegenwärtiger Welt.

105

茅坪港
Maoping Do

双
Double-L

坛子岭
Tanziling Crown
Topfberg

秭归新县城
New Zigui County·
Neue Kreisstadt von Zigui

长江三峡水利枢纽工程
The Three Gorges Key Water Conservancy Pivotal Project
Wasserbauschlüßelprojekt von Drei Schluchten des Changjiang-Flußes

三峡茅坪副坝
Three Gorges Maoping Side-Dam
Strohpllatz von Drei Schluchten

105

乐天溪
Letian Stream
Bach von Optimismus

坝河口
Bahekou
Flußmündung am Damm

黄牛岩
The Yellow Cow Rock
Gelbrindefels

黄陵庙
Huangling Temple
Gelbgrab-Tempel

ock
hleuse

西陵长江大桥
Xiling Yangtze Bridge
Changjiang-Brücke über Westgeabschlucht

105 長江三峡水利樞紐工程航拍
105 A Photo of the Three Gorges Key
Water Conservancy Project Shot in the Air
105 Wasserbauschlüßelprojekt von
Drei Schluchten des Changjiang-
Flußes auf Luftphotographie

106 泄洪
106 Flood Discharge
106 Hochwasserabfluß

■ 長江三峽工程

公元 2003 年 6 月 16 日，三峽工程五級船閘已經通航，6 月底，三峽工程開始發電外送，截止于 2003 年 11 月 22 日，三峽工程創造了一年內裝機 420 萬千瓦，連續投產 6 臺 70 萬千瓦的水電安裝和投產的世界新紀録，并一舉成爲國内裝機容量最大和發電能力最强的大型電站。這標志着三峽工程已進入了收獲期，功在當代，利在千秋！

■ Yangtze Three Gorges Project

On June 16, 2003, the 5-stage ship locks began to open to put into serve. In the end of June, the Three Gorges Project started to generate electricity and transmit electricity outside. By November 22, 2003, the Three Gorges Project had installed generators of the capacity of 4.2 million kW and successively put 6 units generators (the capacity of each unit is 70,000kW) into produce in one year. It updated world records again and has become the largest hydropower station, which has the largest installed capacity and strongest power of generation in our country. This symbolized that the Three Gorges Project has been in the harvest period. "Contribution belongs to present age, benefits will last forever!"

■ Sanxia- Schluchten des Changjiang-Flußes-Projekt

Am 16. Jun. 2003 wurde die fünfstufige Schiffschleuse von Sanxia-Schluchten-Projekt für Schiffahrt geöffnet. Ende Juni diese Jahres beginnt das Kraftwerk mit der Stromerzeugung und Stromausführung. Bis 23. Nov. 2003 hat das Sanxia-Schluchten-Projek damit den Weltrekord angestellt, daß es in einem Jahr eine installiert Leistung von 4,200,000kW gemacht und 6 Generatorenaggregate von 27kW kontinuirlich, montiert und dazu die Installation für Wasser- und Stromanschluß fertiggebracht sowie diese Anlagen in Betrieb genommen hat, wodurch ist es das große Kraftwerk mit der größten installierten Leistung und stärksten Stromerzeugungsfähigkeit in China geworden. Dies kennzeichnet, daß das Sanxia-Schluchen-Projekt schon in die Erntezeit kommt. Verdienste von heute, Günste für der alle Zeiten!

107 雙向五級船閘
107 Double- Lane 5- Stage Shiplock
107 Fünfstufige Zweiwegschiffschleuse

107

107

108 高峡出平湖
108 A Smooth Lake Rising in the High Gorge
108 Flachsee aus Hochschluchten

108

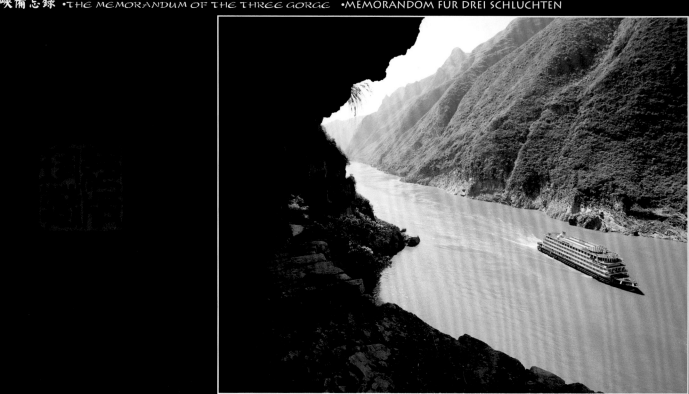

神龍溪 ·SHENNONGXI RIVER · SHENNONG-BACH

作者簡介

Author Brief introduction

Information übe

盧進: 重慶大學畢業, 現爲宜昌市黨風廉政電視教育中心主任、國家二級編劇、中國藝術攝影學會會員。藝術簡歷:

曾編導出版電視作品二十余部, 策劃、撰搞和攝影作品近五十部(集), 其中大型電視文化風光系列片《長江三峽》獲94中泰國際風光大獎賽"金象"銅獎, 大型音樂藝術片《三峽夢》獲中宣部"五個一工程"提名獎, 電視劇《峽口觸礁》獲中紀委優秀黨教片向全國推薦。還應中央電視臺之邀先后成功執導大型電視系列片《長江攬勝》、電視風光片《鬼城豐都》、《清江夢》、《屈原故裏》、《巴人故裏·長陽》等十余部(集)電視作品。

十多年來, 傾情于長江三峽風光的攝影創作, 其攝影作品散見于全國各類報刊、雜志, 由于刻苦鑽研, 成績顯著。2002年5月, 被中國藝術攝影學會和《中國攝影家》雜志社授予"中國優秀攝影家"稱號。2003年與同仁合作航拍三峽, 并出版大型攝影畫冊《長江三峽寫真長卷》, 出版個人作品集大型攝影畫冊《新三峽》。

電話: 0717-6252885

手機: 13907208526

地址: 湖北省宜昌市勝利四路52號

郵編: 443000

Email:lujin8526@162.com

Autor

Lu Jin, graduated from Chongqing University, now is the director of Yichang Television Education center of party conduct and honest administration, national second-level editor, a member of the Chinese Artistic Photography Society. His biographical notes are as follows:

He wrote, directed and published about 20 television works. He plotted, wrote and photographed nearly 50 works. Of these, the large television cultural scenic series the Yangtze Three Gorges won two golden-statue copper prizes of the International Scenic Prize, the large musical artistic play The dream of the Three Gorges was nominated by °∞Five Ones Project°± of the Propaganda Department of the CPC Central Committee, the television play Striking a reef at the mouth of the Three Gorges was conferred the title °∞Chinese outstanding play of party member education°± by the Central Commission for Discipline Inspection of the CPC and recommended to the whole nation. Responding the invitation of CCTV, he successfully directed over ten television works early or late such as the large television series Appreciating the scenery of the Three Gorges, the television scenic plays Ghost Town Fengdu, The Dream of the Qingjiang River, Qu Yuan°Øs Hometown, The Hometown of the Ba Man°™°™Changyang, Talking about the New Three Gorges, and etc. about 10 television plays. He has devoted himself to the photography and creation of the scenery of the new Three Gorges for more than ten years. His works of photography were published on many kinds of newspapers and magazines of the whole nation. Because he studies hard, he achieved remarkable success. May 2002, he was conferred the title °∞Chinese outstanding photographer°± by Chinese Artistic Geography Society and the Chinese Geography Magazine cy. In 2003, his colleagues and he cooperated to take the photos of the Three by air and published the large photo album Long Portrait Volume of the ree Gorges.

Lu Jin, in Chongqing- Universität absolviert, ist jetzt der Leiter der TV-Erziehungszentrale für Arbeitsstil der Partei und redliche der Verwaltung, Dramatiker der zweiten staatlichern Klasse, Mitglied der Chinesischen Gesellschaft für künstlerische Photographie.

Künstlerische Leistungen:

Er hat ca, 20 Drehbücher für Fehensehen verfasst und herausgegeben, ca, 50 Werke (Teilen) geplant, geschrieben und dafür Bildaufnahme gemacht, und davon hat der große TV-Landschaftsseriefilm <<Drei Schluchten des Changjiang-Flußes>> bei dem 1994 China-Tanland-International "Geldelefant" Landschaftsfilmpreis die Bronzemedaille gewonnen, der große Musikfilm << Traum von Drei Schluchten>> bei dem "Fünf Ersten-Projekt" von der Propagandaabteilung beim Zentralkomitee den Kandidaten-Preis gewonnen, und der TV-Spielfilm<< An Schluchtmündung auf Grund stoßen>> wurde von der Disziplinkontrollkommission beim Zentralkomitee als ausgezeichneter Erziehungsfilm für Parteiarbeitsstil landesweit empfohlen. Und er hat noch im Auftrag von Zentral-Fernsehsender mehr als 10 TV-Filmwerken (Teilen) wie den große TV-Seriefilm <<Sehenswürdiger Changjiangfluß>>, den TV-Landschaftsfilm<<Geisterstadt-Fengdu>>, <<Traum von Qingjiang-Fluß>>, <<Heimat von Qu Yuan>>, <<Heimat von Ba-Menschen • Changyang>> usw. früh und später erfolgreich inszeniert.

Seit mehr als zehn Jahren ist er leidenschaftlich für das phtographische Schaffen von Landschaft bei Drei Schluchten des Changjiang-Flußes, und dessen photografische Werke sind in vielen Zeitungen und Zeitschriften im China zu sehen und zu lesen. Da er fleißig und intensiv studiert, hat er so beträchtliche Erfolge erzielt. In Mai 2003 wurde ihm der Titel "Ausgezeichneter Photograph" von der Chinesischen Gesellschaft für künstlerische Photographie und dem Verlag der Zeitschrift<<Photographen in China>> verliehen. 2003 hat er mit seinen Kollegen in Zusammenarbeit die Luftphotographie von Drei Schluchten des Changjiang-Flußes durchgeführt und die große Bildhand <<Realiotische Beschreibung über Drei Schluchten des Changjiang-Flußes>> und individuell das große Bildband<<Neue Drei Schluchten>> veröffentlicht.

圖書在版編目(CIP)數據

新三峽／盧進攝. －北京：中國旅游出版社，
2004.3
ISBN 7-5032-2071-6

Ⅰ.新... Ⅱ.盧... Ⅲ.①風光攝影－中國－現代
－攝影集②三峽—攝影集 Ⅳ.J424

中國版本國書館 CIP 數據核字(2004)第 011575 號

書　　　名：新三峽
作　　　者：盧進
責任編輯：龔威健
裝幀設計：徐牧　朱紅霞　高克平
英文翻譯：王　娟
德文翻譯：深圳市譯博士翻譯公司
編　　　輯：朱紅霞
篆刻題字：蔡静安
地圖繪制：姚一龍
出版發行：中國旅游出版社
地　　　址：北京建國門内大街甲九號
郵　　　編：100005
制作印刷：深圳市精典印務有限公司
開　　　本：889 毫米 X 1193 毫米 1/20
印　　　張：8
版　　　次：2004 年 3 月第一版第一次印刷
印　　　數：(中·英·德) 1－3000 册　0012800

如有印裝質量問題，請與承印廠